Name

11+

Revision
Guide

Sue Hunter

GALORE
PARK

AN HACHETTE UK COMPANY

Photo credits

p23 (l) © klikk – Fotolia **p23 (r)** © andreanita – Fotolia.com

Every effort has been made to trace all copyright holders, but if any have been inadvertently overlooked, the Publishers will be pleased to make the necessary arrangements at the first opportunity.

Although every effort has been made to ensure that website addresses are correct at time of going to press, Galore Park cannot be held responsible for the content of any website mentioned in this book. It is sometimes possible to find a relocated web page by typing in the address of the home page for a website in the URL window of your browser.

Hachette UK's policy is to use papers that are natural, renewable and recyclable products and made from wood grown in sustainable forests. The logging and manufacturing processes are expected to conform to the environmental regulations of the country of origin.

Orders: please contact Bookpoint Ltd, 130 Park Drive, Milton Park, Abingdon, Oxon OX14 4SE. Telephone: (44) 01235 827720. Fax: (44) 01235 400454. Email education@bookpoint.co.uk Lines are open from 9 a.m. to 5 p.m., Monday to Saturday, with a 24-hour message answering service. Visit our website at www.galorepark.co.uk for details of other revision guides for Common Entrance, examination papers and Galore Park publications.

ISBN: 978 1 4718 4923 7

© Sue Hunter 2016

Published by Galore Park Publishing Ltd,

An Hachette UK Company

Carmelite House

50 Victoria Embankment

London EC4Y 0DZ

www.galorepark.co.uk

Impression number   10 9 8 7 6 5 4 3 2 1

Year   2020 2019 2018 2017 2016

Illustrations by Integra Software Services, Ltd.

Typeset in India

Printed in Spain

A catalogue record for this title is available from the British Library.

Contents and progress record

Use this page to plot your revision. Colour in the boxes when you feel confident with the skill and note your score and time for each test in the boxes.

Topics in italic are not included in the ISEB 11+ examination.

3 Chemistry: Properties and uses of materials

	Revised	Score	Time

/32

4 Physics: Forces, light, sound, electricity and space

	Revised	Score	Time

/23

How to use this book

Introduction

This book has been written to help you revise the topics you have covered in Science to help you prepare for your 11+ exam. The book is designed to remind you rather than teach you. It will help you to:

- devise, describe and record experiments clearly
- answer Science questions with confidence on all the topics in the 11+ syllabus
- understand what the examiners are looking for in your answers
- find out how to stand out from the other candidates.

Use the book in the best way to help you prepare. Work through the pages with a parent or on your own, then try the questions and talk about them afterwards. Each topic takes up two pages, which can be studied in half an hour. You are more likely to remember important information if you revise in short bursts rather than spending an afternoon when you are tired, so try setting time aside after school two or three days a week. You may be surprised how quickly you progress.

Pre-Test and the 11+ entrance exams

The Galore Park 11+ series is designed for Pre-Tests and 11+ entrance exams for admission into independent schools (there is currently no pre-test for Science). These exams are often the same as those set by local grammar schools, too. Most schools requiring you to take Science will use the ISEB (Independent Schools Examinations Board) syllabus, although it is possible that if you are applying to more than one school, you will encounter more than one type of test. Either:

- the 11+ entrance exam set by the ISEB
- or 11+ entrance exams created specifically for particular independent schools.

To give you the best chance of success in these assessments, Galore Park has worked with 11+ tutors, independent school teachers, test writers and specialist authors to create this *Revision Guide*.

The content covers the National Curriculum Programmes of Study for Key Stages 1 and 2 as well as the *entire* ISEB 11+ syllabus to the end of Year 6. This content includes the topics studied *after* the ISEB 11+ examinations (so not examined) in January.

Not included in ISEB 11+ exams

All post-January topics are flagged like this paragraph and appear in italics on the contents and progress record pages, so you should be aware of them and thus not surprised if you have not yet covered this material. The reason for their inclusion is that they will be needed when preparing for the 13+ entrance exams, and could potentially occur in bespoke 11+ tests by individual schools.

The learning ladders

You will see these learning ladders appear throughout the Galore Park series. The ladder below shows how the questions progress in Science. Your ability to problem-solve will develop as you step up the ladder, bringing together all your knowledge to solve the most challenging questions by the time you reach the top.

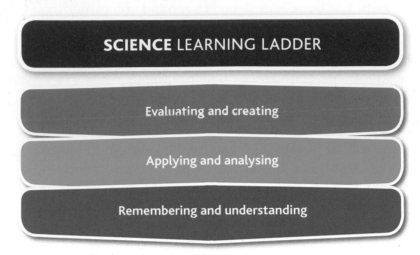

The percentage of each type of question in the tests within this book matches the percentage of each type of question you will come across in the 11+ exams.

Working through the book

The **Contents and progress record** helps you to keep track of your progress. When you have finished one of the learning spreads or tests below, turn back to these introductory pages and complete them by:

- colouring in the 'Revised' box on the planner when you are confident you have mastered the skill
- adding in your test scores and time to keep track of how you are getting on and work out which areas you may need more practice in.

Chapters: the book is divided into four chapters: the first chapter, 'Working scientifically' links to all three following chapters, looking at how scientists work in relation to designing, performing and recording experiments – something you may be asked to do or describe in your 11+ exams. Chapters 2–4 look at the topics you may be tested on in detail.

Chapter introductions: these explain about the different areas of Science. These pages also provide advice for your parents so that they can help you revise with some extra activities.

Learning pages: explain one topic across every two or four pages.

- When answering multiple-choice questions (in these pages and in the tests that follow), make sure that you read and think about all the possible answers before underlining the correct one neatly with a ruler.
- Because many of the questions at the end of these pages will relate to the content you have just read, cover up the learning text before answering the questions; check the content after you have written your answers and then check the answers at the back of the book.

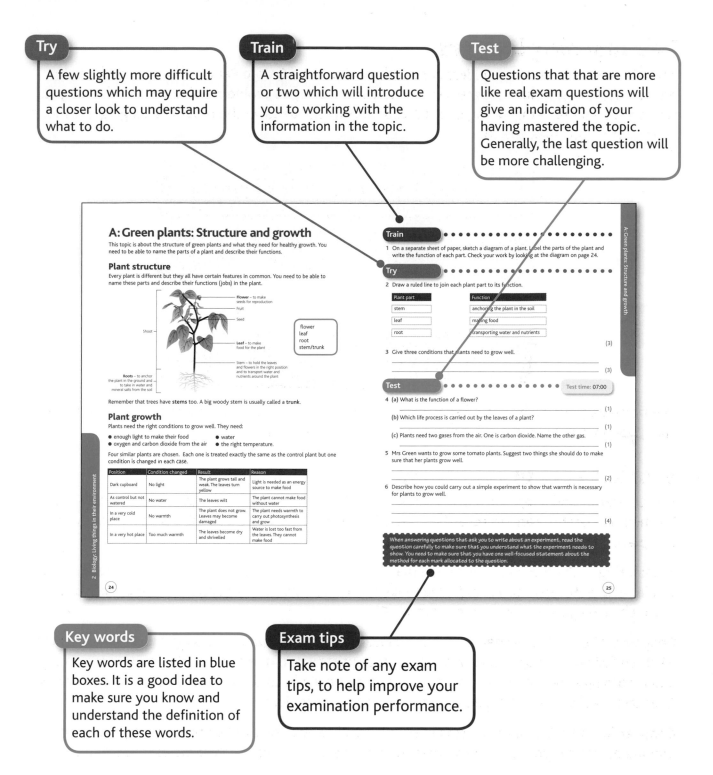

Try

A few slightly more difficult questions which may require a closer look to understand what to do.

Train

A straightforward question or two which will introduce you to working with the information in the topic.

Test

Questions that that are more like real exam questions will give an indication of your having mastered the topic. Generally, the last question will be more challenging.

Key words

Key words are listed in blue boxes. It is a good idea to make sure you know and understand the definition of each of these words.

Exam tips

Take note of any exam tips, to help improve your examination performance.

- **End of chapter tests** give you a chance to practise more questions relating to the topics in the chapter in a short test. The *test time given is for an average test* (some challenging tests are faster). Always time yourself to build up your speed.
  - Complete the test in pencil, aiming for the test time given.
  - Complete the questions you don't finish during the time (but mark down which ones they are).
  - Go through the test again with a friend or parent and talk about the questions you found tricky.
  - Later on, have a second attempt to see if you can improve your time.

● **Answers** to all the tests in the book can be found in the cut-out section beginning on page 117. Try not to look at the answers until you have attempted the questions yourself. Each answer has a full explanation and breakdown of marks so you can understand why you might have answered incorrectly.

Test day tips

Take time to prepare yourself the day before you go for the test: remember to take sharpened pencils, an eraser, protractor, ruler, compasses and a calculator. A watch is very important so you can time yourself. Take a bottle of water in with you, if this is allowed, as this will help to keep hydrated and improve concentration levels. …and don't forget to have breakfast before you go!

For parents

This book has been written to help both you and your child prepare for the 11+ entrance exams. It is designed to help you support your child with clear explanations for parents at the beginning of each chapter, which include:

● tips on the important areas of Science that your child should have mastered
● advice on how additional work can have an impact on success
● activities and games to practise using the skills in enjoyable ways.

The teaching content is designed so that it can be tackled in simple steps. Setting aside time when your child can concentrate fully on one or two topics while you are there to support them can help to make the experience manageable and enjoyable.

All the answers are clearly explained in order to support you and your child in reviewing questions they may have found challenging.

There are a number of topics, as explained, which it is unlikely that your child will have encountered and may not have to cover for the 11+. However, it is worth checking with the schools they are applying to before leaving this content out.

For teachers and tutors

This book has been written for parents and tutors working with children preparing for 11+ entrance exams. All the Year 6 material is covered so that the book is also a useful tool for 13+ revision and for any bespoke tests the children may encounter.

Continue your learning journey

When you've completed this *Revision Guide*, you can carry on your learning right up until exam day with the following resources.

The *Practice Papers* contain six single-subject training tests for Physics, Biology and Chemistry (two for each subject) and six model 11+ papers, replicating the most challenging exams you may encounter. They also include realistic test timings and fully-explained answers for final test preparation. These papers are designed to improve your accuracy, speed and ability to deal with the most challenging questions in exam conditions.

① Working scientifically

What is 'Working scientifically'?

The word *science* means knowledge. When you are revising for exams it seems that there is a lot of material that you have to learn but science is really more about doing than knowing. Our current knowledge and understanding of science has been built up, bit by bit, by scientists observing, measuring and thinking about the world around them. To make scientific investigations useful, we need to know how to do them properly.

Working scientifically is all about how scientists, including you, do science. Scientific investigations start with a question. You need to be able to ask questions in a way that helps you to design a practical investigation and it is always a good idea to try to predict what you think the outcome will be. You need to understand about variables and how they can affect your results. You should be able to measure variables accurately, choosing the correct measuring equipment and you should be able to record your results methodically. When you have obtained your results, you need to be able to say how well they answer your initial question and maybe suggest ways in which your investigation could be improved or extended.

In the 11+ exam you may be asked to:

● describe how a simple investigation might be carried out
● perform calculations (so remember to take your calculator to the exam)
● show data from an experiment in a bar chart or graph. It is important to make sure that you can do this really neatly and accurately as you may also be asked to identify a pattern in the data.

Advice to parents

Questions testing your child's ability to work scientifically are looking for your child to show a methodical approach. The topics in this chapter cover the types of question asked in the 11+ exam and how to answer them successfully. It is always important for your child to read questions carefully to make sure that it is clear what is expected.

When plotting graphs and bar charts, it is important that your child works accurately. Errors in plotting points on a graph can make it hard to answer subsequent questions. Some exercises in this book will require your child to use a sheet of graph paper. Please make sure that this is available for use at home.

'Working scientifically' will not usually be tested explicitly in a separate question. Usually candidates are required to show their ability to use these skills in the context of a wider question. Some questions require a piece of more extended writing, often to describe an experimental procedure. The key to these questions is to look at the number of marks allocated. This shows how many well-focused statements are required to answer the question. Encourage your child to write the key points clearly, using the correct scientific vocabulary and then stop!

A: Variables and questions

Introduction

In science you should always be asking questions. A good question will help you to decide how to set up an investigation. You need to understand about the different types of variable and how to use them.

Variables

Variables, sometimes called factors, are things that can be changed in an investigation. There are three key types of variable:

- The **independent variable** is the thing that you will change in a methodical way during the investigation.
- The **dependent variable** is what will be measured to get the results. You expect it to be affected by (depend upon) what happens to the independent variable.
- **Control variables** are everything else that could possibly change and affect your results. You need to keep these the same throughout the investigation if you are carrying out a fair test.

Asking questions

An investigation question must say clearly what the independent variable and dependent variable will be in your investigation.

"How can I make a parachute fall more slowly?" is fine as a starting point for a project but it is **not** a good investigation question because there are lots of things that might slow the parachute.

"How does the area of the parachute affect the time it takes the parachute to fall?" is a much better question. It is clear that you are going to try several different sizes (the independent variable) and measure the time taken to drop (the dependent variable).

Train •

1 By each of these questions write **Yes** or **No** to show whether they are good investigation questions.

(a) What happens to the height a squash ball bounces if we use different surfaces?

Yes

(b) What is the best fabric for making a tent? *No*

(c) How does the mass on a brick affect the force needed to make it move?

yes

(3)

2 Fill in the table to show the independent variable and the dependent variable for each investigation.

Question	Independent variable	Dependent variable
How does the temperature of the room affect how quickly seeds germinate?	✓	
What happens to the distance travelled by a car if the height of the ramp is increased?		✓
Does the size of a magnet affect how many paper clips it can pick up?		✓

(6)

11

B: Units, measurement and working safely

It is really important for you to measure variables accurately. You need to know which units are used to measure the different variables and you need to be able to identify the most appropriate measuring device.

Units

You must always state the units used whenever something is measured.

The units used for variables in 11+ examinations are as follows:

Variable	Units used
length	metre (m), kilometre (km), centimetre (cm) or millimetre (mm)
area	m^2 or cm^2
volume	m^3 or cm^3
mass	gram (g) or kilogram (kg)
temperature	degrees Celsius (°C)
force	newton (N)

It is worth remembering a few useful measurements. You can then use these to help you to estimate other values. For example:

- The temperature of a healthy human body is 37 °C. You can estimate other temperatures by seeing if things feel hotter or cooler than your hand. (Be careful doing this though!)

- The mass of an apple is about 100 g.

- The height of a table is usually about 75 cm.

Measuring devices

It is important to select the correct measuring device. Sometimes there are different sizes of measuring device. You should always try to choose the one that is closest to the value being measured, as this will give the most accurate answer.

The devices you will need to know about are as follows:

Variable	Measuring device used
length	ruler, tape measure or trundle wheel
volume of liquids	measuring cylinder
mass	balance
temperature	thermometer
force	force meter (newton spring balance)

Some measuring devices have a digital display so it is easy to read the value. Others have a scale and the value is shown by a pointer. Exam questions sometimes ask you to read a value from a scale. Remember to look carefully at the scale before you take the reading. Make sure that you know what each little division on the scale is worth and then count them carefully to get the correct reading.

Safety

In science many activities can be dangerous. You need to make sure that you take care to prevent harm to you and other people.

Here are some basic safety rules:

- Wear goggles or safety glasses, especially when handling or heating chemicals.
- Wash your hands after handling chemicals, animals, plants, soils, etc.
- Wipe up any spills immediately.
- Never leave a flame, such as a candle or a Bunsen burner, unattended.

In the exam you might be asked to suggest safety precautions that should be taken when doing a particular investigation. Think carefully about the activity concerned and what risks might be involved. Then suggest sensible precautions that should be taken to minimise the risks.

Train

1 What units would be most appropriate to use to measure the following items?

(a) the mass of an apple _gram_

(b) the volume of a solution _m³_

(c) the force taken to lift your pencil case _N_

(d) the width of the classroom _m_

(e) the length of a ladybird _mm_ (5)

2 Peter is given two force meters. One measures from 0 – 10 N and one measures from 0 – 100 N. Which should he choose to measure as accurately as possible the force taken to pull a block (roughly 9 N)? Explain your answer. _____ (2)

3 Read the values shown on the scales.

(a) _____ (1)

(b) _____ (1)

C: Testing

There are a number of different types of investigation. You should be able to suggest what type of investigation is the best to answer a question. You may also be asked to describe briefly a possible method for an investigation.

Types of investigation

The type of investigation that you are most likely to be asked about is a **fair test**. Fair tests are used to answer the kind of questions described in topic A.

In a fair test you need to change one variable, measure one variable and keep all of the other variables the same.

In some investigations we have one part of the experiment that will be used as a comparison with the results of other parts. We call this a **control**. An example is the investigation into seed germination in Chapter 2 Topic A, where a control set of seeds is grown with water, oxygen, warmth and light. The other tests each remove one condition and the germination is compared with the control.

Not all investigations can be done by fair testing. Sometimes the best way to find the answer to a question is to observe and record what you see. For example, comparing the types of invertebrates found in a wood and in a field or finding out about the changes in a tree during a year.

Repeating readings

It is a good idea to repeat readings when doing an investigation. This allows you to **check your results** to see if they are **reliable (repeatable)**. To get one result at the end, we find the mean (average) of the repeated readings. If the results are not very reliable, this process gives a better answer than a single reading.

> If asked why readings are repeated, do not fall into the trap of saying that it is to make it a fair test. Repeating an unfair experiment will never make it fair.

Planning an investigation

Sometimes exam questions ask you to describe a method for an investigation.

It is a good idea to read the whole question through again carefully to make sure that you know what question the investigation is answering. Then think about how the experiment could be done to answer the question.

Look at the number of marks for the question. This will give you the number of clear points you need to include. You might describe:

- what would be changed (independent variable)
- what would be measured (dependent variable)
- any key variables to be controlled
- what apparatus you would use and how (but keep it brief).

You should not need to write any more than can be fitted into the space provided, so think carefully about what you want to say and keep it simple but clear. Use scientific vocabulary whenever you can as this helps to reduce the amount you need to write.

Train

1 Rebecca wants to find out whether the floor surface affects the distance travelled by a toy car after it has run down a ramp.

(a) What is the independent variable in her investigation (= what will she change)?

The angle of the ramp _____ (1)

(b) What is the dependent variable in her investigation (= what will she measure)?

_____ (1)

(c) Suggest two things she would need to keep the same to make it a fair test. (Remember to focus on things that would affect the result.)

A flat surface and 90° ramp _____

_____ (2)

2 Tamal wants to find out if the size of sugar crystals affects how quickly they dissolve. He puts the sugar into a beaker of water. He stirs the mixture and uses a timer to find out how long the sugar takes to dissolve.

What would Tamal need to do to make this a fair test?

One sugar crystal and 1 minute time _____

_____

_____ (4)

3 Describe how you could carry out an investigation to find out whether the length of people's legs affects how quickly they can run.

First you have to get to people then meauser the legs lengther and make them run to see hoo is the fastest. _____

_____ (4)

4 Some children want to make a catapult. They have some different widths of elastic and they want to find out which is best for the catapult.

(a) What might they choose as their dependent variable?

The size of the catapult _____ (1)

(b) If they choose this variable, what question are they investigating?

which can catapult the longest. _____ (1)

D: Recording results 1: Tables and bar charts

Scientists collect lots of data when they carry out experiments. Data must be recorded in an organised way, in a form that everyone can understand. You should be able to draw up a simple table to record your results and fill it in correctly. You should also be able to show your results in the form of a bar chart or line graph if appropriate.

Results tables

Tables of results are almost always drawn up according to a simple set of rules:

- Tables have two or more columns or rows.
- The independent variable is always in the first (left-hand) column or the top row.
- The dependent variable is recorded in the right-hand column or second row.
- If readings are repeated there may be more than one column or row, one for each repeated reading and one for the mean (average).
- Units are always written in the heading of the column or row and not with each reading.

For example, how does the **volume of a sound** (dependent variable) change as the **distance from the sound source** (independent variable) increases?

Distance of sensor from sound source, in metres	Volume of sound, in decibels

Displaying results in a bar chart

Bar charts and graphs are useful to make it easier to interpret the results of an investigation.

Bar charts

The features of a good bar chart:

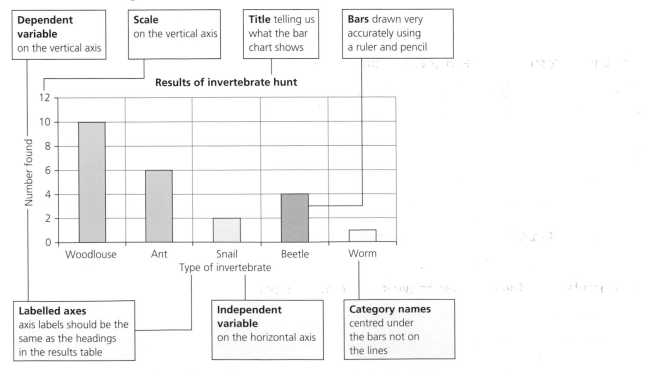

In an 11+ exam you will always be told whether to draw a bar chart or a graph so read the question really carefully to make sure that you draw the right one.

In the exam you might be asked to add any of the features from the diagram here to a grid or partially drawn bar chart.

When drawing bars on a bar chart in the exam the accuracy of your bars is what matters. Use a ruler and a sharp pencil and check the scale carefully before drawing the top of your bar. Draw the sides of the bar as well. Make sure that your lines are neat but clearly visible. It is not necessary to colour the bars in. This uses up time that would be better spent answering other questions.

Train

1 Edward hangs a spring from a bar and fixes a cup on the end. He adds marbles to the cup. Each time he adds a marble, he measures the length of the spring. He records his results in his notebook.

> 0 marbles = 5.0 cm, 1 marble = 5.4 cm, 2 marbles = 5.8 cm

In the space below, record Edward's results in a suitable table.

(4)

2 The table shows the results from an investigation.

Position of bird feeder	Number of birds in 15 minutes
Near house	2
Woods	10
Lawn	5

The bar chart shows some of these results.

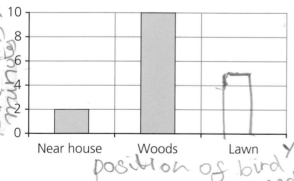

position of bird feeder

(a) Label the axes on the bar chart.   (2)

(b) Complete the bar chart by drawing in the missing bar.   (1)

(c) Suggest a suitable title for this bar chart.

position of bird feeder house.   (1)

E: Displaying results 2: Plotting graphs

Graphs are another way to show your data. A graph is made up from accurately plotted points and generally has a line or curve added to show the pattern in the results.

You will need some graph paper for the questions at the end of this topic.

Drawing graphs

The features of a good graph:

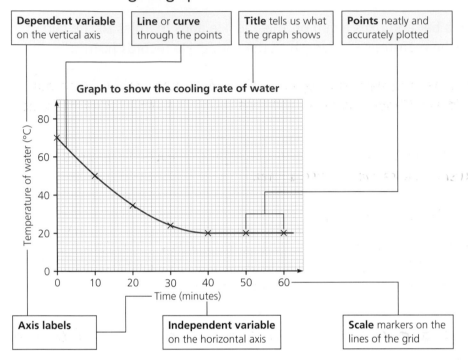

| **Dependent variable** on the vertical axis | **Line** or **curve** through the points | **Title** tells us what the graph shows | **Points** neatly and accurately plotted |

Graph to show the cooling rate of water

| **Axis labels** | **Independent variable** on the horizontal axis | **Scale** markers on the lines of the grid |

You could be asked to add any of the features here to a grid or partially plotted graph.

Plotting a point on a graph

Points on a graph need to be plotted accurately. To do this:

1 Find the value of the independent variable from the results table.

Mass added to spring, in g	Stretch of spring, in cm
0	0
100	4
200	8

2 Locate this value on the horizontal axis.

3 Find the value of the dependent variable from the results table.

4 Locate this value on the vertical axis.

   Keep this graph somewhere safe as you will need it for the questions on page 21.

5 The point should be plotted at the meeting point of the vertical line representing the value of the independent variable and the horizontal line representing the value of the dependent variable.

6 Mark the point with a small, neat cross, using a sharp pencil.

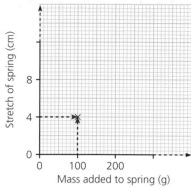

Drawing the line

You may be asked to draw the line at any stage during a question. Make sure that you read the question carefully so that you do exactly what is asked. When drawing the line, look carefully at the pattern shown in the data.

Is it a straight line? If so, **use a ruler** for the line. If it is not a straight line you will be asked to **draw a smooth curve through the points**. Do not use a ruler.

Points that do not fit the pattern

When a graph has been plotted, it is usually easy to see the general pattern in the data. Sometimes one point clearly does not fit the pattern. If this is the case, you will be asked to draw a ring around it. This point must not be included when you draw the line.

Train

The table shows the results of an investigation into how the diameter of a parachute affects the time taken for it to fall.

Diameter of parachute, in cm	Time taken to fall, in seconds
10	1.7
20	2.0
30	1.8
40	2.7
50	3.0

1 On a sheet of graph paper, draw two neat axis lines. Label the axes with the independent variable on the horizontal axis and the dependent variable on the vertical axis. Add the scale to each axis. (4)

2 Plot the points carefully. (4)

3 One of the points does not fit the pattern. Draw a circle around this point on your graph. (1)

4 Draw a straight line through the rest of the points. (1)

> Remember to read every word of all questions. Sometimes a 'question' is an instruction to do something, such as add the axis titles to a bar chart. There will not be an answer line to write on, so make sure that you do not lose marks by missing out this type of question.

F: Interpreting graphs

Introduction

Once you have drawn your graph, you may be asked to use it to provide answers to further questions.

Reading values from a graph

A graph can be used to predict other values. In the exam, the question may ask you to **use your graph** to find the value. Do not try to guess the answer by looking at the data in the results table. You must read the value accurately from the graph and show how you have done so by drawing lines on the graph.

For example:

To use the graph to find the mass of substance that would dissolve at 25 °C:

1 Locate 25 °C on the horizontal axis.

2 Use a ruler and pencil to draw up the 25 °C line until you meet the graph line.

3 Draw along the horizontal line from here until you meet the vertical axis.

4 Read the value on the vertical axis (22 g).

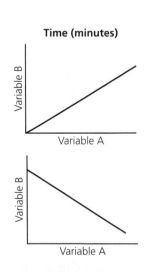

The same technique can be used in the opposite direction, in this case to find the temperature at which a given mass of solvent would dissolve.

Describing the pattern shown by the line

You may be asked to describe the pattern shown by the results. Your answer should explain what happens to the dependent variable as the independent variable changes. You can work this out by looking at the line.

The line on this graph slopes up towards the right. This shows us that, as the independent variable (Variable A) was increased, the dependent variable (Variable B) also increased. For example, as the mass added to the spring increases, the length of the spring increases.

The line on this graph slopes down towards the right. This shows us that, as the independent variable (Variable A) was increased, the dependent variable (Variable B) decreased. For example, as the time increases, the temperature of the water decreases.

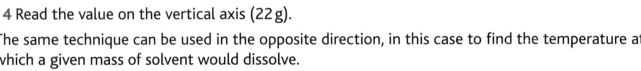

> If the line is a curve, it will probably show a similar pattern to the two examples just discussed but look at it carefully because some curved lines may rise and then fall, or fall and then rise.

Train •

1 (a) Use the graph you drew for the Train activity in topic E to find out how long a parachute with a diameter of 35 cm would take to fall. Show your working on the graph.

_____

(3)

(b) What pattern is shown by the line of the graph?

horstinel
_____

_____

(2)

2 The graph lines show changes in temperature during some experiments. In each case, describe what happens to the temperature as the time increases.

(a)

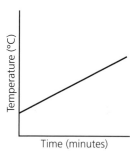

_____

_____ (1)

(b)

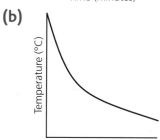

_____

_____ (1)

(c)

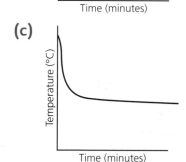

_____

_____ (2)

2 Biology: Living things in their environment

What is biology?

Biology is the study of living things. This chapter is all about plants and animals, including humans, and the places where they live.

Biologists study plants and animals by careful observation, looking for similarities and differences and trying to work out how these help living things to survive. To be a good biologist, you need to be observant and to think about the world around you.

All living things need a place to live, and the place where they live is called their habitat. To do well in the 11+ exam you need to think about the conditions in different habitats and the plants and animals that live there. You should think about how a habitat changes over time and how the animals and plants cope with these changes. You should learn about what animals eat and how they get their food, and how they mate and rear their young.

It is important for you to understand how animals and plants rely on each other and on the food, water and shelter provided by the habitat. This will help you to say what people might do to make sure that human activities do not harm the natural world.

Advice to parents

To succeed in biology questions in the 11+ exam, your child needs to develop an awareness of the natural world and the plants and animals that live in it. There are so many living things and habitats in the world that it is quite possible that an 11+ question requiring the application of acquired knowledge will focus on something that has not been directly studied in class. Such a question does not require factual knowledge of the animal, plant or habitat; rather it is testing understanding of the general principles of interdependence, adaptation, etc. that have been learnt.

It can be very helpful to relate the concepts in this chapter to the natural world in the place where you live or maybe a place shown in a programme you watch together on the television, encouraging a sense of enquiry and closer observation of the familiar. You could look for similarities and differences between plants and animals and encourage discussion as to how these might help the animals and plants that live in the habitat to survive.

You might also discuss how the day-to-day activities of your family might impact on the other living things in the area and how this impact might be minimised.

Setting the scene: Life processes

This page helps you to prepare for your 11+ exam by thinking in different ways about important processes that are common to all living things.

Life processes

Biology is the study of living things. How can we tell if something is alive or not?

Look at these two bears.

1 In what ways are these two bears similar and how do they differ? On a separate sheet of paper, describe as many similarities and differences as you can.

> To make your work clear when describing similarities and differences, make sure that you include both items. For example, if comparing a brown bear and a polar bear, you might say, 'They both have fur covering their bodies. A brown bear has brown fur but a polar bear has white fur.'

All living things carry out certain activities to stay alive. We call these **life processes**. Three important life processes that you need to recognise are **nutrition** (feeding), **movement**, **growth** and **reproduction**.

The teddy bear does not eat and it cannot move by itself. It will never get any bigger and it cannot mate to make more teddy bears. It is not alive. The brown bear carries out all these life processes because it is a living thing.

> growth
> life processes
> movement
> nutrition
> reproduction

2 What would happen if brown bears did not carry out the life processes? Fill in your ideas in the spaces below.

If brown bears did not ...

Feed	Move	Grow and reproduce
on fiish and salmons they be instinged	The will have be dead and they will be safe to touch	They will be very mery scard and scared big things.

A: Green plants: Structure and growth

This topic is about the structure of green plants and what they need for healthy growth. You need to be able to name the parts of a plant and describe their functions.

Plant structure

Every plant is different but they all have certain features in common. You need to be able to name these parts and describe their functions (jobs) in the plant.

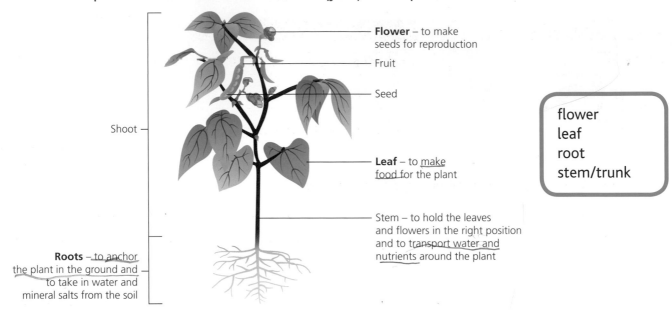

Flower – to make seeds for reproduction

Fruit

Seed

Shoot

Leaf – to make food for the plant

Stem – to hold the leaves and flowers in the right position and to transport water and nutrients around the plant

Roots – to anchor the plant in the ground and to take in water and mineral salts from the soil

flower
leaf
root
stem/trunk

Remember that trees have **stems** too. A big woody stem is usually called a **trunk**.

Plant growth

Plants need the right conditions to grow well. They need:

- enough light to make their food
- oxygen and carbon dioxide from the air
- water
- the right temperature.

Four similar plants are chosen. Each one is treated exactly the same as the control plant but one condition is changed in each case.

Position	Condition changed	Result	Reason
Dark cupboard	No light	The plant grows tall and weak. The leaves turn yellow	Light is needed as an energy source to make food
As control but not watered	No water	The leaves wilt	The plant cannot make food without water
In a very cold place	No warmth	The plant does not grow. Leaves may become damaged	The plant needs warmth to carry out photosynthesis and grow
In a very hot place	Too much warmth	The leaves become dry and shrivelled	Water is lost too fast from the leaves. They cannot make food

Flower structure

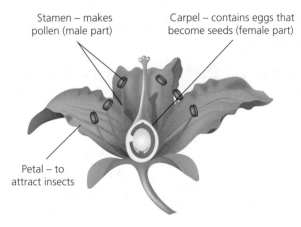

Stamen – makes pollen (male part)

Carpel – contains eggs that become seeds (female part)

Petal – to attract insects

Remember that wind-pollinated flowers do not have bright petals because they do not need to attract insects.

Train

2 On a separate sheet of paper sketch a diagram of a flower and label it. Check that your diagram and labels match the ones just discussed.

Stages of the plant life cycle

Pollination takes place when pollen is transferred from the stamen of one flower to the carpel of another by insects or the wind.

germination
pollination
seed dispersal
seed formation

Seed formation happens when the pollen joins with eggs inside the carpel and the eggs become seeds. The carpel becomes a seed case or fruit.

Seed dispersal is the name given to the process of seeds spreading to new places to avoid competition for light and water. Seeds are mostly dispersed by wind or animals but a few are dispersed by floating on water. Seed cases are adapted for a particular type of seed dispersal. Seeds that are dispersed by the wind have wings or parachutes on their seed cases. Seed cases of seeds dispersed by animals provide food for the animal or have hooks to catch on the animal's coat.

> Make sure that you do not confuse wind pollination with seed dispersal by wind.

Germination takes place when a seed begins to grow. The root grows first to anchor the plant and take in water. Food stored in the seed provides energy until the first leaves grow.

Seeds need the right conditions to germinate. They need:

> You can remember the conditions a seed needs to germinate with the acronym 'WOW!'

● water
● oxygen from the air
● warmth.

We can show that water, air (oxygen) and warmth are necessary by sowing some seeds in four test tubes. In test tube A the seeds are given all three conditions. This is the control.

The germination of these seeds will be compared to the seeds in the other test tubes. In tubes B, C and D, one of the conditions is removed.

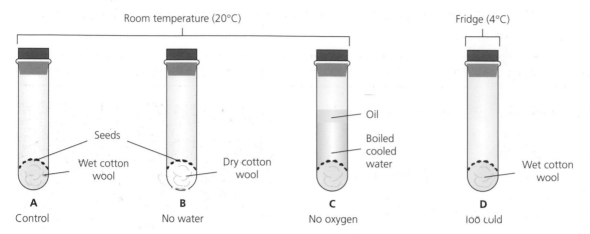

Room temperature (20°C)   Fridge (4°C)

Seeds
Wet cotton wool   Dry cotton wool   Oil
Boiled cooled water   Wet cotton wool

A   B   C   D
Control   No water   No oxygen   Too cold

Only the seeds in test tube A will germinate.

Train

3 On a separate sheet of paper, list the four main stages in the life cycle of a plant. Add a brief description of what happens at each stage.

Try

4 Tick three boxes to show what a plant needs to make food by photosynthesis.

water ☑   carbon dioxide ☑

oxygen ☑   light ☑   (3)

5 (a) Where in a plant would you expect to find the green pigment called chlorophyll?
      in a grass feilded _____ (1)

   (b) What is the function of chlorophyll?
      Transporting water and nutrans. _____ (1)

6 Underline the word that best completes the following sentences:

   (a) The part of a flower that makes pollen is the

      A carpel   B petal   C stamen   D stem

   (b) A condition that seeds do **not** need for germination is

      A light   B oxygen   C water   D warmth   (2)

7 Explain why it is important for seeds to move away from the parent plant before germinating.
      It won't have space _____ (1)

8 Use words from the box to complete the following sentences. Each word may be used once, more than once or not at all.

| asexual | carpel | germination | insects | pollination | stamen | wind |

(a) Brightly coloured petals on a flower attract
_____*asexual*_____ .

(b) In the process called *pollution*
_____*germination*_____ grains of pollen
from the _____*germination*_____
of one flower are transferred to the
_____*carple*_____ of another by
_____*insectey*_____ or the _____*wind*_____ .

> When you answer questions using words from a box, do not cross out the words when you use them. You may need to use some words more than once.

(c) New plants can sometimes be made from pieces of root or stem. This is called
_____*germination*_____ reproduction. (7)

9 Explain why photosynthesis is important to

(a) plants _*if it was not important nothing put water will be on this world.*_ (1)

(b) animals _*Ther won't be animals ether on this beatful magnificent world.*_ (1)

10 A biologist finds the seed of a new plant.

(a) Suggest how this seed might be dispersed.
*The seed will exploed its container* (1)

(b) Explain your answer.
*because the seed exploed and the root will get out* (2)

11 Mr Hunter planted some bean seeds in two different places in his garden.

He noticed that the seeds in one place germinated more quickly than the ones in the second place.

Suggest two reasons why these seeds might have germinated more quickly.

1 _*the positining.*_

2 _*the watering time*_ (2)

C: Feeding relationships and adaptation

This topic covers the different ways in which animals obtain their food. You need to know how living things link together in food chains and the words used to describe living things at each level in the chain. You also need to know about some of the ways in which animals and plants are adapted to help them to obtain food.

Obtaining food

All living things need food to give them the energy and materials that they need for activity and growth.

carnivore
consumer
herbivore
omnivore
predator
prey
producer

Different living things obtain food in different ways:

- Plants make their own food. We call these **producers**.
- Animals are **consumers**. They find and eat (consume) food from plants or other animals.

There are different types of consumer:

- **Herbivores** only eat plants.
- **Carnivores** only eat meat from other animals.
- **Omnivores** eat plants and meat.
- **Predators** catch and eat other animals, which are known as **prey**.

Adaptations for feeding

You may be asked to describe ways in which a pictured plant or animal is adapted to help it to obtain food or to stop itself being eaten.

Look out for the following features:

- Plants: large leaves to help them to take in light for photosynthesis.
- Predators: sharp teeth, beaks or claws to help them to hold onto their prey.
- Prey animals: camouflaged to help them to hide from predators. Shells, spines or poison to protect them from predators.

Food chains

All food chains start with a producer (plant) because they are the only living things that can trap energy from the Sun and turn it into food energy (see topic B). For example:

| oak leaf | → | caterpillar | → | blue tit | → | sparrowhawk |
| producer | | herbivore | | carnivore | | top carnivore |

> Remember that the arrows in a food chain show how the energy passes from the food to the consumer. You can help yourself to remember by reading each arrow as 'is eaten by'.

Food chains in 11+ questions

You may be asked to write a food chain from a habitat that you have studied. It is a good idea to make sure that you have prepared a food chain for a habitat that you have visited or learnt about in school.

Sometimes you need to write a food chain using information given in the question. Remember to look back at the whole question, including any pictures, to find the information you need.

Try

1 Cheetahs hunt antelopes to eat. Antelopes eat grass. Write a food chain to show this information.

(3)

2 Brown bears eat fish, small animals and fruit and seeds. What word is used to describe an animal feeding in this way?

food cahin (1)

Test

Test time: 09:00

3 Here is some information about some animals found in a woodland habitat.

Animal	Food
tawny owl	mice, birds, young rabbits
badger	small animals, seeds, soft fruit
fox	small animals, birds
chaffinch	mainly seeds
mouse	nuts, seeds, soft fruit

(a) Use the information in the table to write **two** food chains.

1 _small anmdtis_ → _bidles_ → _fox_
2 _seed_ → _soft fruit_ → _small/animls._ (6)

(b) Using information from the table, name one living thing that is:
  - a predator _loin_
  - an omnivore _humen & beans_
  - a herbivore. _Cattiplen_ (3)

4 Here is a picture of a golden eagle.

Golden eagles catch mammals and birds. Describe two ways in which the golden eagle is adapted for hunting its prey and state how these help it to catch its food.

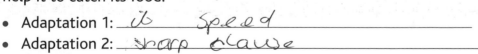

  - Adaptation 1: _its speed_
  - Adaptation 2: _sharp claws_ (2)

5 Explain why plants are known as producers.

There are the fist thing in the food chaing (1)

D: Habitats

This topic covers plants and animals in their habitats. You need to know what a habitat provides and about how plants and animals are adapted to survive in their habitats.

Habitats

A habitat is the place where a plant or animal lives. The habitat must provide:

- food and water
- shelter
- a safe place to breed.

Different habitats have different conditions. Animals and plants need to have special adaptations to survive the conditions in their habitat. Here are some examples.

Desert

Hump stores fat so the camel can survive without food for several days

Long eyelashes to keep sand out of its eyes

Thick fur helps keep the camel warm at night and cool during the day; camel does not sweat until its body temperature reaches over 40 °C to reduce water loss

Large flat feet to stop the camel sinking into the sand

Pond

Eyes on the top of the head to allow the frog to see above the water whilst still submerged

Thin moist skin to absorb oxygen from the water, camouflaged body to hide from predators

Long sticky tongue for catching insects

Large webbed feet for swimming

Long, strong back legs for jumping to escape danger

Conditions in a habitat change during the day and between seasons. Animals have special behavioural adaptations to these changes.

> hibernate
> migrate
> nocturnal

- Some are **nocturnal** so they hunt and feed at night when it might be safer or cooler.
- Some **hibernate**. They sleep through the cold winter months when food is scarce.
- Some **migrate**. They travel long distances to find food or suitable breeding grounds.

Train ●●●●●●●●●●●●●●●●●●●●●●●●●

1 You may need to be able to describe an animal from a habitat that you have studied. On a separate sheet of paper, describe its size and shape, how it moves, what it eats and some ways in which it is adapted to survive in that habitat.

Try

2 Draw ruled lines to join each word to the correct meaning.

Words	Meanings
migrate	sleep through the winter
hibernate	active at night
nocturnal	travel long distances in search of food or breeding grounds

(2)

3 Rainforest monkeys have long tails. Suggest one way in which these might help them to survive in the rainforest.

hibernate ___ (1)

Test

Test time: 07:00

4 What is meant by the term 'habitat'?

were an amilies good at ___ (1)

5 Dormice are small mammals that live in woodland.

(a) Name three things that the woodland habitat must provide for the dormice.

food , shelter and space ___

___ (3)

(b) Small mammals find it hard to survive in very cold weather. Suggest two ways in which the dormice might survive the winter.

1 dig go in a hole ___

2 dig a hole. ___ (2)

6 Lucy notices that the church tower is home to some bats.

Bats hang head down in the church tower to sleep during the day and hunt for their insect prey at night. They locate the insects by making high-pitched squeaks and listening for the reflected sounds.

(a) What word is used to describe animals that are active at night?

hibernate ___ (1)

(b) Suggest why the bats locate their prey using sound.

So they now wich way to go ___ (1)

(c) Suggest one way in which it might be an advantage to the bat to be active at night.

there eye ___ (1)

E: Human impact on the environment

In this topic you will look at ways in which human activity affects the environment and the animals and plants that live in it. You should be able to describe some harmful effects of human activity. You should also be able to describe ways in which humans can have a positive impact on the environment.

Harmful effects of human activity on the environment

Humans have much more impact on the environment than other animals. For example:

- **Pollution** (adding materials to the environment that should not be there).
  - Gases from vehicles, factories and power stations pollute the air. Waste from factories and sewers pollutes waterways. Rubbish pollutes the land.
  - Pollution damages habitats and kills plants and animals. Some gases in the air trap heat and are thought to be causing the climate to become warmer.
- **Habitat destruction** (changing a habitat so that it is no longer suitable for the plants and animals that lived there).
  - Cutting down forests for farmland. Building towns and cities on fields and open countryside.
  - When habitats are destroyed the living things have to try to find somewhere else nearby to live and this is often not possible.

Some types of plants and animals become very rare due to the effects of human activity. They may become **endangered** (very few left so in danger of dying out) or **extinct** (none left).

> endangered
> extinct
> habitat destruction
> pollution

Beneficial human actions

Humans can help the environment by:

- using fewer resources, including fuel and materials for making things
- using renewable sources of energy, such as using wind, sunlight or waves to make electricity. This reduces pollution and slows down the rate at which we use up fossil fuels
- recycling used materials so that we create less waste and use fewer of the Earth's resources.

Humans can help living things by:

- protecting areas of habitat, especially where endangered species live, to give them the best possible chance of breeding successfully
- restoring damaged habitats and joining up habitat areas to allow animals to move more freely to feed and find mates
- breeding very rare species in captivity and releasing them when the habitat is safe for them.

Try

1 What is meant by the term 'pollution'?

_____ (1)

2 People are encouraged to recycle as much as possible. How does recycling our used materials help the environment?

_____

_____

_____ (2)

Test

Test time: 05:00

3 Tigers are an endangered species. Human activity has destroyed much of their habitat.

(a) Describe one way in which human activity may harm a habitat.

_____

_____ (1)

(b) What is meant by the term 'endangered species'?

_____

_____ (1)

(c) Suggest one way in which humans might help tigers to survive.

_____ (1)

4 An increasing amount of our electricity comes from renewable resources.

(a) Name two renewable energy resources.

_____ and _____ (2)

(b) Describe one way in which the use of renewable energy helps the environment.

_____ (1)

5 Farmers often leave a strip of uncultivated land around the edges of their fields. Suggest one way in which this might help farmland wildlife.

_____ (1)

F: Animal life cycles

This topic covers the life cycles of some different animals. You need to be able to describe the differences between the life cycles of a mammal, an amphibian, an insect and a bird.

What is a life cycle?

A life cycle shows how an animal or plant carries out the life process of reproduction.

A life cycle can be shown as a diagram. Here is the life cycle of a frog.

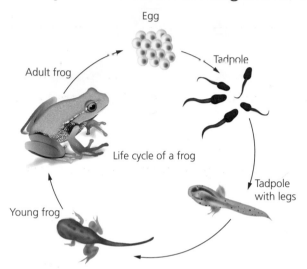

Egg

Tadpole

Adult frog

Life cycle of a frog

Tadpole with legs

Young frog

egg
fertilisation
fuse
gestation period
metamorphosis
sperm

Similarities between life cycles

- Most animals require two parents to reproduce. This is called sexual reproduction.
- The female parent produces **eggs** and the male parent produces **sperm**.
- To make a baby an egg and a sperm must **fuse** (join) together. This is called **fertilisation**.
- The baby needs a period of time to grow before it is ready to mate and produce babies of its own.

Comparing life cycles

Mammals: Field mouse

The babies grow within the mother's body. This is called the **gestation period** and varies in length between animals, from a few days to as much as 660 days for an elephant. The gestation period for a mouse is about 21 days. The mother cares for the young and feeds them on milk.

Amphibians: Frog

Most amphibians lay eggs in water. The young (tadpoles, sometimes known as larvae) do not look like the parents. They have tails to swim with but no legs. They live in the water and breathe through gills. The parents do not care for their young. The tadpoles then undergo a big change, called **metamorphosis**, into the adult form. They lose their tails and grow legs. They breathe with lungs. Most adult amphibians live mostly on land.

Insects: Butterfly

The female lays eggs on a plant. The babies (caterpillars or larvae) do not look like the parents. They feed on leaves for a few weeks. The parents do not care for their young. When the caterpillars have grown big enough they find a safe place and turn into a pupa. Inside the pupa the caterpillar undergoes metamorphosis and emerges as an adult butterfly.

Birds: Robin

The female lays hard-shelled eggs in a nest. The parent birds will sit on the eggs to keep them warm until the babies are ready to hatch. The parents feed the young on insects until they are ready to leave the nest.

Try

1 (a) What is meant by the term 'sexual reproduction'?

This means that most mammels need two parents to (2) _repreduse,_ (worn)

(b) What is meant by the term 'fertilisation'?

To make a baby an egg and a sperm must ffuse together. (1)

2 What name is given to the time during which baby mammals grow within their mother's body?

The name of this proccess is called gestation period (1)

3 Most birds lay their eggs in early summer. Suggest a reason why this might be a good time for birds to rear their young.

I think this is a good time becauze it can keep the egg warm. (1)

Test

Test time: 06:00

4 Describe one similarity and one difference between the life cycles of a mammal and a bird.

Similarity: _____

Difference: _Mammals don't grow feathers But birds do_ (1)

5 (a) Amphibians undergo a big change during their life cycle. What word is used to describe this big change?

Metamorphosis (1)

(b) For a named amphibian that you have studied, describe how the animal changes during this time.

Name of amphibian: _Frog_

Changes: _They have a tail when they are young but they don't have a tail when they are a adult._ (3)

6 (a) Amphibians lay hundreds of eggs in a pond when they breed. Suggest one advantage of laying so many eggs.

They might have room. (0)

(b) Suggest one disadvantage of laying so many eggs in one place.

They need space when they hatch. (1)

they

37

G: Human life cycle

This topic is about how humans reproduce. You need to know about the main stages in the human life cycle and about the main changes that occur during adolescence.

The human life cycle

adolescence
fetus
periods

A human **fetus** (developing baby) grows in its mother's body for about 9 months (40 weeks).

After the baby is born it is fed on milk for several months and needs a lot of care from its parents. As human children grow they learn many new skills and become more independent. **Adolescence** is the time when humans change from children into adults.

Once they become adults, humans can find a partner and, when they feel ready to do so, they can have children of their own. Older humans may still be very active, perhaps helping to look after grandchildren for example, but may need more care as they reach the end of their lives.

Adolescence

Adolescence, sometimes called puberty, is the time when girls and boys become adults. During adolescence a number of changes happen in the human body. Some of these are shown in this table.

Both boys and girls	Girls	Boys
Growth spurt	Hips become wider	Shoulders widen
Hair develops under the arms and around sex organs	Breasts develop	Hair grows on the face
Moodiness	**Periods** start (menstruation)	Voice becomes deeper
Spots may develop on the face		Penis and testes become bigger

Adolescent boys and girls often begin to care more about their appearance and what other people think of them. Adolescence occurs at different times in different people. Some may start noticing changes at 8 years old; others may not start changing until they are 13 or 14 years old.

Try

1 Underline the word or phrase that best completes the following sentences.

(a) The gestation period of a human baby is about

    A   6 months   B   9 months   C   12 months   D   24 months   (1)

(b) The time when a child becomes an adult is called

    A   adolescence   B   gestation   C   growth   D   senescence   (1)

2 Rewrite the following stages in the human life cycle in the correct order, starting with the youngest.

| adolescent | adult | baby | child | fetus |

_____E Fetus, Baby, child, & adolescent and Adult._____ (4)

Test   Test time: 05:00

3 Give an example of a change that takes place during adolescence in

(a) girls only: __Periods start__ (1)

(b) boys only: __Pinis and testes become bigger__ (1)

(c) girls and boys: __None__ (1)

4 (a) A human baby takes about 40 weeks to develop inside its mother's body. How many days is this? __280 days__ (1)

(b) The gestation period of a mouse is about 21 days and that of an elephant is about 660 days. Suggest how long the gestation period of a chimpanzee might be. Explain your answer.

__I might be the 280 days, same as humans__
__because chimpanzees are really close to us.__ (2)

5 People often live for a long time after their children have grown up. Suggest one reason why this might be helpful to human society.

__Old people have more wisdom the to help the__
__human society.__ (1)

$$\begin{array}{r} 40 \\ \times\ 7 \\ \hline 280 \end{array}$$

eg need space when they hatch.

H: Evolution and inheritance

This topic covers how plants and animals change over long periods of time to make new species. You also need to know how the study of fossils, living plants and animals helps scientists to understand these changes.

The fossil record

Scientists called **palaeontologists** study fossils (see Chemistry topic F) to find out about the life forms that lived millions of years ago. They can tell how old fossils are by where they are found in the layers of sedimentary rocks. This allows them to see that **species** have changed over time. Some species have gradually changed to form the animals and plants we know today. Others were not able to survive when their habitats changed and they became extinct.

> palaeontologist
> species

Mary Anning was a palaeontologist who discovered many important fossils in the rocks near Lyme Regis in Dorset. She was the first to discover *Ichthyosaurs*, *Plesiosaurs* and *Pterodactyls*. Her discoveries and those of other scientists made people realise that species could change to make new species but they didn't know how.

Differences between individuals

Most animals and plants have two parents. Every individual has some characteristics that are inherited from each of its parents. All the offspring will be the same species as their parents but each one will be slightly different.

Differences lead to adaptation

Sometimes a small difference can make an animal or plant better able to survive in its habitat. This individual will then be stronger and healthier and more likely to mate.

Some of the offspring of this individual will inherit the beneficial change. They too will survive better and pass the change on to their offspring. Over a number of generations this change will become widespread and the species will have become better adapted to its habitat. For example, arctic foxes developed thicker fur to keep them warm and giraffes developed longer necks to reach leaves high up in trees.

Adaptation can lead to evolution

Sometimes the changes that occur over time make the animal or plant so different that a new species is created. This is called **evolution**.

> evolution

The processes leading to evolution were worked out by Charles Darwin and Alfred Wallace who observed species of animals and plants on different islands. They both realised that new species had been created as the living things adapted to the different conditions on each island.

Selective breeding

Farmers and animal breeders use the changes in individuals to create new varieties of animals and plants with particular characteristics. They choose the individuals with the best characteristics in each generation to breed from. Over time the good characteristics are seen in more and more individuals of the breed. This is also how wolves have changed, over thousands of years, into all the different breeds of dog alive today.

Try

1 (a) A scientist who studies fossils is called a

    A biologist   B geographer
    C palaeontologist   D parasitologist

(b) Changes resulting in the formation of a new species are called

    A adaptation   B alteration
    C evolution   D separation   (2)

2 Explain one way in which scientists can work out the age of a fossil.

_____

_____ (2)

Test

Test time: 06:00

3 Explain how the study of fossils helps scientists understand evolution.

They can find it out when where the fossils are found in the layers of sedementry Rocks. (1)

4 (a) Describe how differences can occur between individuals of a species.

They don't look same.

_____ (1)

(b) Explain how these differences might lead to the formation of a new species.

_____

_____

_____ (3)

5 Describe briefly how a farmer might use selective breeding to create a variety of sheep that produces thicker wool.

_____

_____

_____ (3)

I: Classification of plants and animals

This topic looks at how plants and animals can be divided into groups with similar characteristics. You should be able to describe the distinguishing characteristics of the groups mentioned in this topic.

Why classify?

Scientists put things into groups with similar characteristics to make it easier to study them. All living things are given a two-part Latin name according to a system devised by Carl Linnaeus. People in every country use the same names to avoid confusion.

Grouping living things

All living things can be placed into one of five large groups, called 'kingdoms'. These are:

1 plants
2 animals
3 fungi
4 single-celled organisms (protists)
5 bacteria.

> Remember that fungi are not classed as plants because they do not contain chlorophyll and cannot carry out photosynthesis.

Classifying plants

Plants are placed in one of two groups:

1 Flowering plants that make seeds for reproduction.
2 Non-flowering plants that do not make seeds, such as ferns, mosses and seaweeds.

Classifying animals

Animals are divided into two types:

1 **Vertebrates:** these are animals with an internal skeleton.
2 **Invertebrates:** these are animals without an internal skeleton.

> invertebrate
> vertebrate

Vertebrates

There are five vertebrate groups and you need to be able to describe the distinguishing characteristics of each of them.

Group	Warm or cold blooded	Body covering	Reproduction	Other
1. Mammals	Warm	Fur	Young develop in mother's body.	Babies fed on milk.
2. Birds	Warm	Feathers	Hard-shelled eggs.	Wings
3. Amphibians	Cold	Moist skin	Jelly-covered eggs laid in water.	Can breathe through skin.
4. Reptiles	Cold	Dry scaly skin	Soft-shelled eggs laid on land.	
5. Fish	Cold	Scales	Eggs laid in water.	Breathe with gills.

> If asked how you know that an animal belongs to a particular group, describe characteristics that are special to that group (diagnostic features) and not found in other groups. For example, only mammals have fur and feed their young on milk so these features are diagnostic. Size is not a diagnostic feature as animals in any group can be different sizes.

Invertebrates

One group of invertebrates is the **arthropods** (animals with a hard outer case called an exoskeleton and jointed legs). These include the insects and the spiders. You should be able to describe the differences between these sub-groups:

- Insects have 3 pairs of legs, 3 parts to their bodies and may have wings.
- Spiders have 4 pairs of legs, 2 parts to their bodies and do not have wings.

The other arthropods are the **crustaceans** (crabs, lobsters, woodlice) and the **myriapods** (centipedes and millipedes).

Other invertebrate groups include **molluscs** (slugs and snails) and **worms**.

Try

1 Explain why fungi are not classified as plants.

_____ (1)

2 **(a)** What do all vertebrates have in common?

_____ (1)

(b) Name the five vertebrate groups.

_____ (5)

Test

Test time: 04:00

3 Some children are studying extinct creatures. They see a picture of a mammoth. James says that the mammoth was a mammal. What evidence is there in the picture to show that he is correct?

_____ (1)

4 Describe two differences between insects and spiders.

1 _____

2 _____ (2)

5 Lizards and newts look quite similar. Lizards are reptiles and newts are amphibians. Suggest how you could tell the difference between a lizard and a newt.

_____
_____ (2)

Keys

Keys are used to help us to identify the living things that we find. Keys are based on the important differences between types of animal or plant that can be used as diagnostic features. To use a key you need to be observant and make comparisons between living things.

There are two types of key: branching keys and number keys.

Branching keys

In a branching key you work your way down by answering a series of yes/no type questions and following a trail through the key. Here is an example of a branching key to identify invertebrates.

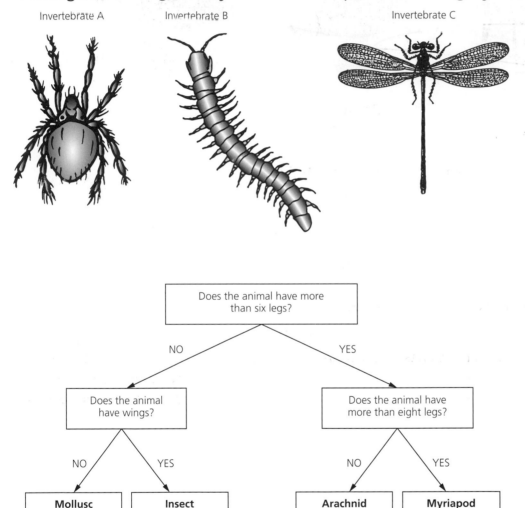

Invertebrate A   Invertebrate B   Invertebrate C

Look carefully at Invertebrate A. The first question is 'Does the animal have more than six legs?' The animal has eight legs so the answer is 'Yes'. Follow the YES arrow to the next question, 'Does the animal have more than eight legs?'. The animal has eight legs so the answer here is 'No'. Follow the NO arrow and you find that the animal is an arachnid.

> You may be asked to suggest a question to complete a key. Look for one difference between the two items that can be clearly seen in the pictures.

Number keys

In a number key, you are given a pair of choices at each numbered step. At the end of the line with the correct choice the key tells you which step to go to next. It is important to read **both** lines of each question carefully before deciding which to pick. Here is an example of a key to identify water birds.

(A) 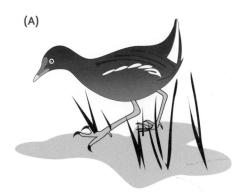   (B) 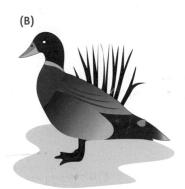   (C)

1 The bird has a short neck	Go to 2	
The bird has a long neck	Go to 4	
2 The bird has a tuft on its head	**great crested grebe**	
The bird has a smooth head	Go to 3	
3 The bird has webbed feet	**mallard**	
The bird does not have webbed feet	**moorhen**	
4 The bird has a white neck	**swan**	
The bird has a black neck	**Canada goose**	

Look carefully at Bird A. Read both lines of question 1. The bird has a short neck so we follow the instruction at the end of the first line and go to question 2. The bird has a smooth head. The instruction at the end of this line sends us to question 3. The bird does not have webbed feet so it is a moorhen.

Try

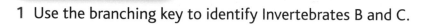

1 Use the branching key to identify Invertebrates B and C.

_____ (2)

2 Follow the number key to identify Birds B and C.

_____ (2)

3 Use the branching key to identify the following animal tracks.

A

B

C

D

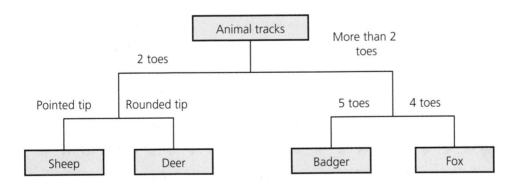

A _____

B _____

C _____

D _____

(3)

4 Use the number key to identify the following winter twigs from common trees.

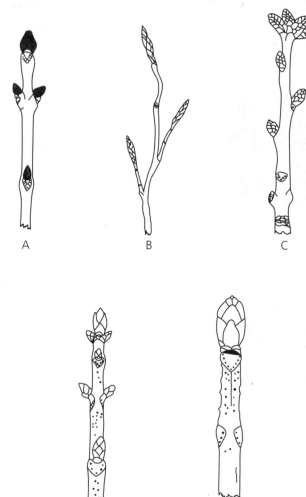

A   B   C

D   E

1	The twig has a single bud at the tip	Go to 2
	The twig has more than one bud at the tip	Go to 4
2	The buds are very thin and pointed	**beech**
	The buds are rounded	Go to 3
3	The buds are black	**ash**
	The buds are not black	**horse chestnut**
4	The buds at the tip are all the same size	**oak**
	One tip bud is larger than the others	**sycamore**

A _____

B _____

C _____

D _____

E _____

(4)

K: The human body

This topic is about what is found inside the human body. You need to know the functions of the skeleton and the names of the major bones. You also need to be able to identify some important organs in the body.

Skeleton

Our skeleton has three functions: it supports the body, protects important organs and helps with movement. Without a skeleton, humans would not be able to stand up or move around in the same way. Our bodies would be too big to support themselves.

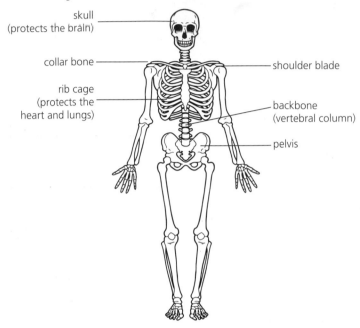

skull
(protects the brain)

collar bone

rib cage
(protects the
heart and lungs)

shoulder blade

backbone
(vertebral column)

pelvis

Moving the body

The body moves when muscles **contract** and **relax**. In vertebrates the muscles are attached to the bones. The skeleton provides a framework for movement. In animals without skeletons, muscles pull on soft body parts or on a hard exoskeleton.

contract
relax

Not included in ISEB 11+ exams

Bones come together at joints. Muscles move the joints by contracting and relaxing. Each joint is moved by one or more pairs of muscles working in opposite directions (antagonistic muscles).

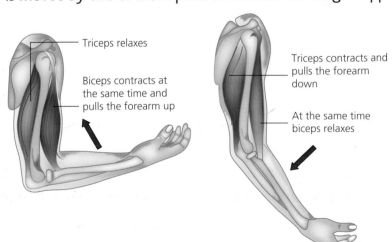

Triceps relaxes

Biceps contracts at
the same time and
pulls the forearm up

Triceps contracts and
pulls the forearm
down

At the same time
biceps relaxes

To raise the hand the biceps contracts and the triceps relaxes. To lower the hand the triceps contracts and the biceps relaxes.

Organs

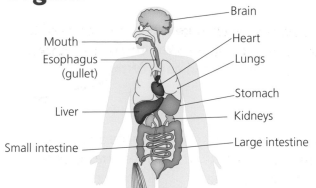

The mouth and teeth, esophagus (gullet), stomach, small intestine and large intestine make up the digestive system which breaks food down, making it ready to be used by the body.

Try

1 Give two important functions of the skeleton.

1 _____

2 _____ (2)

2 (a) Where in the human body would you find the brain?

_____ (1)

(b) Which two organs are found inside the rib cage?

_____ and _____ (2)

Test

Test time: **06:00**

3 Name the bones labelled A, B, C and D on the diagram.

A _pelvis_____

B _backbone_____

C _Sholder blade_____

D _colhr bone_____ (4)

4 Worms are invertebrates but snakes are vertebrates. Suggest one way in which the movement of worms and snakes is different.

_____ (2)

5 Suggest two ways in which life would be different for humans if they did not have a skeleton.

1 _____

2 _____ (2)

L: Teeth and nutrition

In this topic you need to know about the different types of teeth and how to care for your teeth. You should be able to name the nutrients making up a healthy diet and why they are needed by our bodies. You should be able to name at least one food that is rich in each of these nutrients.

Types of teeth

There are four types of tooth.

canine
incisors
molars
pre-molars

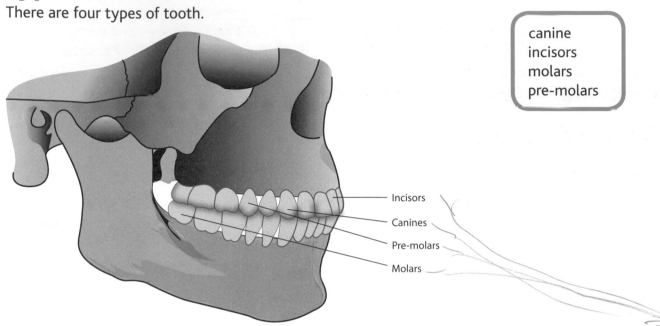

Incisors
Canines
Pre-molars
Molars

You can find out about an animal's diet by looking at its teeth:

- Herbivores have strong incisors to cut leaves and stems and big molars and pre-molars to grind up tough plant material. They usually have no canines.
- Carnivores have sharply pointed teeth. They have long, strong canines for catching prey and tearing meat.
- Omnivores have all the different types of teeth to cope with different types of food.

Caring for your teeth

Plaque is a layer of bacteria on the surface of your teeth. Bacteria change sugars into acid. Acid eats away at the hard enamel surface of a tooth and may make a **cavity** (hole).

To keep your teeth healthy:

- Brush your teeth at least twice a day to remove the plaque.
- Use fluoride toothpaste to strengthen the enamel.
- Visit the dentist regularly.
- Avoid foods and drinks with a lot of sugar in them.

cavity
plaque

Nutrients and a healthy diet

Your **diet** is all the food and drink that you take in. **Nutrients** are substances in the diet that are needed to provide energy for activity, matter for growth and repair and substances needed for healthy growth and to prevent disease. A **balanced diet** is one that contains all the necessary nutrients in the right quantities to keep you healthy.

balanced diet
diet
nutrient
fibre

Nutrient	Needed for	Foods rich in this nutrient
Carbohydrate (starch & sugars)	To provide energy. Glucose is a type of sugar. Most of your energy should come from starch.	Starch: bread, pasta, rice, potatoes Sugars: fruit, biscuits, cakes, sweets
Fat	To store energy and to keep us warm. Too much fat causes heart disease and obesity.	Meat, fish, dairy products, nuts
Protein	To build cells for growth and repair.	Meat, fish, eggs, cheese, nuts, lentils
Vitamins	To prevent disease. Vitamin C prevents scurvy.	Fruits and vegetables. Oranges and lemons are a good source of vitamin C.
Mineral salts	To keep the body functioning properly. Calcium salts are needed for healthy growth of bones.	Dairy products are good sources of calcium.

A healthy diet also contains **fibre**, found in fruits, vegetables and wholemeal bread, to keep food moving through the digestive system. Water is also needed to keep your body hydrated.

Testing for starch

Not included in ISEB 11+ exams

To test a food for starch, add **iodine solution**. If starch is present the iodine will turn from **orange-brown** to **blue-black**.

Try •

1 Name the four different types of teeth.

_____ (4)

2 Name the nutrients described below:

   (a) Prevents scurvy _____ (1)

   (b) Provides energy for activity _____ (1)

   (c) Needed for growth and repair of body cells _____ (1)

Test • • • • • • • • • • • • • • • • •   Test time: 05:00

3 **(a)** What is meant by the term 'balanced diet'?

_____ (1)

   (b) Fat is one of the nutrients that make up our diet.

   (i) Give one reason why fat is necessary in our diet.

_____ (1)

   (ii) Describe one problem that may be caused by eating too much animal fat.

_____ (1)

4 **(a)** What is plaque?

_____ (1)

   (b) Give two ways in which you can keep your teeth healthy.

   1 _____

   2 _____ (2)

M: The heart and circulation

This topic covers why the circulation of blood around the body is important. You should know about the structure and function of the heart, the different types of blood vessels and how exercise affects the heart and keeps it healthy.

Blood

Blood moves around the body through blood vessels.

- **Arteries** carry blood away from the heart.
- **Veins** carry blood towards the heart.

Blood has many functions, including:

- carrying water, oxygen and nutrients around the body
- carrying carbon dioxide and other waste away from the cells
- helping to fight disease.

To do these things it needs to be moved around to reach every organ in the body.

artery	pulse point
contract	pulse rate
glucose	respiration
obesity	stamina
oxygen	vein

The heart

The function of the heart is to pump the blood around the body.

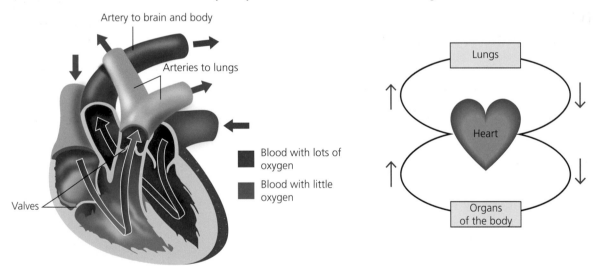

Artery to brain and body

Arteries to lungs

Blood with lots of oxygen

Blood with little oxygen

Valves

Lungs

Heart

Organs of the body

The heart is a strong muscle surrounding four chambers, two on each side.

On each side, the blood enters the upper chamber from a vein. The heart muscle **contracts** so that the blood is pushed down into the lower chamber through a one-way valve. The next contraction pushes the blood out of the heart through an artery. The diagram on the right shows the route taken by the blood around the body.

Exercise and the heart

Your **pulse rate** is a measure of how many times in each minute your heart contracts (beats) to push blood round the body. You can feel your pulse at **pulse points** in your neck or wrist. Your resting pulse rate is probably about 60–80 beats per minute.

Respiration is the life process that cells use to release energy. The materials needed for respiration are **glucose** (an energy source) and **oxygen** to release the energy. These are carried around the body in the blood. When you take exercise, you are using up energy more quickly than if you are resting. Your cells need to be provided with glucose and oxygen more quickly so your heart beats more quickly and your pulse rate increases. When you stop exercising your pulse rate will gradually return to the resting rate.

Health benefits of exercise

Exercise:
● strengthens the heart muscle
● helps to prevent **obesity**
● increases **stamina**.

Try

1   Underline the correct word from each pair to complete the following sentences.

   (a) Blood vessels carrying blood towards the heart are called (**arteries/veins**).

   (b) When you take exercise your pulse rate (**decreases/increases**).   (2)

2   Name two substances, carried in the blood, that are needed by cells to provide energy.

   _____ (2)

Test

Test time: 05:00

3   **(a)** What is the function of the heart?

   _____

   (b) How many chambers are there in the heart? _____ (1)

4   Add arrows to the diagram to show the direction taken by the blood as it moves around the body.

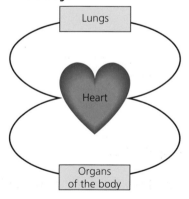

(2)

5   Explain briefly how you could show that your pulse rate increases when you take exercise.

   _____

   _____

   _____ (4)

N: Lungs and breathing, smoking and other drugs

Not included in ISEB 11+ exams

This topic looks at the lungs and how they work. You also need to know how smoking damages the lungs and the effects of nicotine, alcohol and other drugs on the body.

The lungs and breathing

You have two **lungs** and they are found inside the ribcage. The lungs take in **oxygen** from the air and pass it to the blood stream. They also remove **carbon dioxide** from the blood and pass it out into the air.

breathe
carbon dioxide
lung
oxygen

The two gases pass in and out of the lungs through the surface of the lungs and the walls of the tiny blood vessels running across the surface of the lungs. The surface of the lungs is made up of lots of folds to create a large area across which the gases can be exchanged.

> *Do not confuse breathing (taking air in and out of the lungs) with respiration (using oxygen to release energy from glucose in the body cells).*

The air that we **breathe** in (inhaled air):

- contains more oxygen
- contains less carbon dioxide
- is drier and cooler

than the air that we breathe out (exhaled air).

Smoking

Smoking harms the lungs and other parts of the body.

- Tar in tobacco smoke covers the lung surface, reducing the area across which gases can be exchanged. This causes severe difficulty with breathing.
- Smoking can lead to lung diseases including lung cancer.
- Smoking causes fatty blockages in arteries that can lead to heart disease.

Addictive drugs

Drugs are chemicals that affect the body in some way. Most drugs are potentially very harmful.

addictive   medicine
alcohol   nicotine
drug   solvent

Medicines are drugs that can be used to cure or help us to fight disease. They are safe if taken exactly according to the instructions given by a doctor or printed on the packet.

Addictive drugs are substances that are hard to stop taking once you start putting them into your body. Tobacco smoke contains an addictive drug called **nicotine**. **Solvents** are liquids used to dissolve substances to make them ready for use. Some solvents have a strong smell and evaporate easily. The vapour from solvents can be addictive. It causes severe damage to the lungs and brain and can kill. Other addictive drugs include marijuana, cocaine, heroin and ecstasy. These drugs cause damage to many different parts of the body, including the brain.

Alcohol is also a drug that can become addictive. Alcohol interferes with the ability to think sensibly. In excess it may make people become bad-tempered and aggressive and can result in unconsciousness. The next day, someone who has drunk too much alcohol will feel unwell (have a hangover). Alcohol causes damage to the liver, which is an important organ with many functions, including cleaning some poisons out of the blood.

Try

1 (a) Which gas is taken in from the air in the lungs? _____ (1)

  (b) Which life process in the body uses this gas? _____ (1)

2 (a) Name the addictive substance found in tobacco. _____ (1)

  (b) Give two ways in which alcohol can affect people.

    1 _____

    2 _____ (2)

Test

Test time: 05:00

3 How are the lungs adapted to increase the rate of gas exchange?

_____

_____ (2)

4 (a) Tobacco smoke contains tar. Explain how the tar causes breathing difficulties.

_____

_____ (2)

  (b) Give one other harmful affect of tobacco smoke on the body.

_____ (1)

5 Cocaine is an addictive drug.

  (a) What is meant by the term 'addictive'?

_____ (1)

  (b) Give one way in which drugs such as cocaine cause harm to the body.

_____ (1)

O: Micro-organisms

Not included in ISEB 11+ exams

This topic is about micro-organisms. You need to know about the ways in which micro-organisms can cause disease and what can be done to prevent this. You need to be able to name some diseases caused by the different types of micro-organism. You also need to know about some ways in which micro-organisms can be helpful.

Types of micro-organism

Micro-organisms (sometimes called microbes) are living things that are too small to be seen without a microscope. There are three types of micro-organisms:

- bacteria
- viruses
- fungi.

Harmful micro-organisms

Some micro-organisms are harmful.

- Bacteria and viruses reproduce very well in the warm, moist environment of the body, so one bacterial cell or virus can become millions very quickly and cause diseases.
- Bacterial diseases include sore throats, food poisoning, whooping cough, typhoid and infections in wounds.
- Viral diseases include colds, flu, measles, chickenpox and HIV/AIDS.
- Some fungi (moulds) cause food to spoil.

Preventing and curing disease

Many diseases are passed from person to person by touch or through the air.

| antibiotic | hygiene |
| antiseptic | vaccination |

To reduce the spread of disease we need to practise good **hygiene**:

- At a personal level, e.g. washing our hands before eating, after using the toilet and after handling animals.
- At home, e.g. cleaning surfaces, especially in the kitchen and bathroom with an **antiseptic** solution.
- At a community level, e.g. efficient disposal of rubbish, and cleanliness in hospitals and doctors' surgeries.

Antibiotics can be used to treat bacterial diseases but they do not work for viral diseases. This is why a doctor will not prescribe antibiotics for a cold or flu.

Many viral diseases can be prevented using **vaccination**. This involves putting a small amount of harmless viral disease material into the blood. Special cells, called antibodies, are created by the body to fight the disease. These stay in the body so they are ready to fight the disease at any time.

Helpful micro-organisms

Some micro-organisms are helpful.

- Bread, wine and beer are all made using yeast, a type of fungus.
- Cheese and yoghurt are made using bacteria.
- Fungi and bacteria (decomposers) break down dead plant and animal material in the environment, clearing it away and recycling nutrients.

Try

1 What is a micro-organism?

_____ (1)

2 Name the three types of micro-organism.

_____ (3)

3 Name one disease caused by bacteria and one disease caused by viruses.

Bacterial disease: _____

Viral disease: _____ (2)

Test

Test time: 05:00

4 Edward Jenner showed that a disease called smallpox could be prevented using vaccination. He put a small amount of a very similar disease, called cowpox, into a scratch on the arm of a young boy. He later exposed the boy to smallpox but he remained healthy. Explain how this process prevented the boy from developing smallpox.

_____

_____ (2)

5 When you visit a hospital, you are encouraged to clean your hands using an antiseptic gel. Explain why this is a good idea.

_____ (1)

6 Yeast makes bread rise. In the right conditions, yeast carries out respiration and the carbon dioxide creates bubbles in the bread dough. Some children made some bread dough and put a small amount in measuring cylinders. They could measure how much the volume of the dough increased over time.

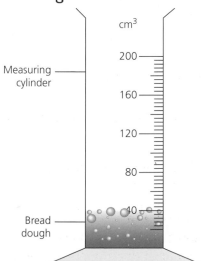

Describe how they could use this method to find the best temperature for yeast to respire. Remember to say how they would make their investigation a fair test.

_____

_____

_____

_____ (4)

Test 1 Biology

1 Underline the word or phrase that best completes the following sentences.

   (a) An animal that eats only plant material is called

   A a carnivore   **B** a herbivore   **C** an omnivore   **D** a vegetarian

   (b) The first living thing in a food chain is always

   A a carnivore   **B** a consumer   **C** a predator   **D** a producer   (2)

2 Write words in the gaps to complete the following passage.

   All the food and drink that we take in forms our _____ . We need to eat a variety of foods to provide all the _____ _____ we need to remain healthy.

   Carbohydrates are a good source of _____ . There are two types of carbohydrate, starch and _____ . We should get most of our energy from _____ .   (5)

3

Bony orbit

Temporomandibular joint

Mandible

B

A

   Look at the picture of a skull.

   (a) Name the two types of tooth shown by the labels.

   A _____   B _____   (2)

   (b) Is this skull more likely to have come from a carnivore or a herbivore? Explain your answer.

   _____

   _____ (2)

4 Peter says that he thinks that plants will grow better the more light they receive.

   (a) Tick one box to show the term that best describes Peter's statement.

   A   a conclusion   ☐

   B   a prediction   ☐

   C   a result   ☐   (1)

Peter decides to carry out an investigation to find out how differences in light levels affect the growth of plants.

(b) What is the independent variable in this investigation?

_____ (1)

(c) Describe how Peter could carry out this investigation.

_____

_____

_____

_____ (4)

5 Alfie and Paul looked at a tall tree. The tree had purple leaves. Alfie said that the tree had no chlorophyll in the leaves. Paul thought that the leaves must contain chlorophyll. Who do you think was right? Explain your answer.

_____

_____

_____ (3)

Record your score and time here and at the start of the book.

Score [   ] / 20   Time [   ]:[   ]

③ Chemistry: Properties and uses of materials

What is chemistry?

Chemistry is the study of materials and their properties. Understanding how materials behave in different circumstances allows people to design and make new things and create new materials.

The world around us is full of things. Some of these are natural and some are man-made. Everything you can see, including yourself, is made up from materials. We could say that materials are the 'stuff' from which things are made.

If we want to make something, we need to choose the best material to make it from. To do this, we need to think about what our object needs to be able to do and choose materials that behave in the right way to make it from. For example, a tent needs to be made from a fabric that is light so that it can be easily carried and flexible so that it can be folded up, and waterproof so that it does not let the rain in. In the exam you might be asked to identify which materials have been used to make something and suggest why they were chosen. To do this well, you need to be able to spot the properties of some common materials and understand why they might be chosen to be used for specific tasks.

Materials change over time. Sometimes that change is very slow and you might not notice it happening, for example the weathering of rocks. Sometimes you might notice changes taking place slowly, for example fruit ripening. Sometimes a change is very fast indeed, for example a gas explosion. You need to be able to answer questions about some of these changes and how they lead to the formation of new materials. Read the question carefully because you may find that important information is given to help you to answer the question well.

Advice to parents

In chemistry your child needs to be able to think about the nature of materials and how they change. Many changes result in the formation of new substances that are very different from the starting materials. This can seem a bit like magic. At 11+ the study of chemistry focuses largely on familiar materials and changes that your child will have experienced in everyday life. As with all science, the key to success is to develop understanding by being observant and thinking about what you notice.

You can help your child become more familiar with materials and their properties by looking at familiar objects and discussing what they are made from and why. Questions in the 11+ exam are often set in the context of everyday situations. Encourage your child to observe everyday changes, such as clothes drying on the line, cooking, fruit ripening or concrete setting, to help build awareness of how principles learnt in the classroom can be applied to real life.

Setting the scene: Properties of materials

Materials are what things are made from. Each material has different properties and the choice of material for a particular use will depend on its properties. In the exam, you might be asked to identify what material has been used to make a particular item and say why it was chosen.

Properties

There are many different properties of materials. All materials have several different properties. You need to be able to identify which properties make a material suitable for its purpose. Here are some key properties that you might come across. Make sure that you know what each of these terms means.

A material might be:

- metal/non-metal
- strong/weak
- hard/soft
- rigid/flexible
- waterproof/not waterproof
- magnetic/non-magnetic
- thermal conductor/thermal insulator
- transparent/translucent/opaque
- electrical conductor/electrical insulator
- cheap to produce/expensive to produce.

The properties needed in a material for making electrical wiring, for example, would be: good electrical conductor, strong, flexible and not too expensive.

1 Choose one object in the room where you are now. On a separate sheet of paper write down the object, the material(s) used to make it and why you think these might have been chosen. Try to think of an alternative material that could have been used. Then think of a really silly choice and say why this would not work.

Thinking about properties: Thermal insulation

Materials that are good thermal insulators do not allow heat energy to pass through them easily whereas thermal conductors do allow heat to pass through them.

Trapped air is a good thermal insulator. For example, the fluffy filling in winter jackets or duvets, double glazed windows and layers of fur or feathers on animals.

Metals are good thermal conductors.

2 On a separate sheet of paper, draw labelled diagrams to show how you could set up a fair test to compare two materials to see which one is the better thermal insulator. Remember to show how you would measure your dependent variable.

A: States of matter

Substances (matter) exist in three states: **solid**, **liquid** or **gas**. You need to know about the properties of these three states and how some materials can change between states. In the 11+ exam you might be asked to draw diagrams to show how the particles are arranged in solids, liquids and gases.

States of matter

All **matter** is made up from tiny **particles**, too small to be seen even with a microscope. We can explain the properties of the states by thinking about how these are arranged. This principle is called **particle theory**.

gas	particle
liquid	particle theory
matter	solid

State	Solid	Liquid	Gas
Arrangement of particles	Particles packed in a regular pattern, vibrating	Particles in irregular arrangement, able to move past each other	Particles widely spaced and free to move
Does it flow?	no	yes	yes
Does it keep its shape?	yes	no, takes the shape of the bottom of the container	no, takes the shape of the container
Does it keep its volume?	yes	yes	no, fills the container

Changing state

Many materials are able to move from one state to another when heated or cooled. Changes of state are **reversible**. They change the form of materials but do not create anything new so they are described as **physical changes**.

boil	melt
condensation	physical changes
evaporation	reversible
freeze	

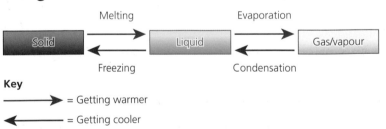

Key
→ = Getting warmer
← = Getting cooler

Changes of state happen at special temperatures. These are different for different substances. The temperature at which a material changes between the solid state and the liquid state is called its **melting point**. This is also known as its **freezing point**.

Evaporation can occur at any temperature when surface particles have enough energy from wind or heat to escape as a gas. Boiling only occurs at the temperature, called the **boiling point** of the liquid, when all of the particles have enough energy and the liquid changes state to gas.

Water

The freezing point of pure water is 0 °C. When water freezes, it expands (gets bigger). This can cause pipes to burst or rocks to crack. Salt on the roads lowers the freezing point of water to prevent the formation of ice.

The boiling point of pure water is 100 °C. Impurities in water may raise its boiling point.

Changes of state and the water cycle

Water is found in all three of its states; it is solid in ice and snow, liquid in seas, lakes and rivers and in the air as a **vapour**. Changes of state of water make up the water cycle.

vapour

Train

1 Draw a diagram on a separate sheet of paper to show the water cycle. If you cannot do one from memory, look it up. Label your diagram to show where water is evaporating and condensing. Try to include freezing and melting as well. Check that you can describe how the water moves through the cycle.

Try

2 Name the three states of matter.

Solid, liquid and ga (3)

3 Describe one difference between the properties of solids and liquids.

Solid is hard liquid is not hard. (2)

Test

Test time: 07:00

4 Explain why droplets of liquid water may be seen on a window on a cold day.

it is cold and fog (gas) a everywhere. and (2)

5 (a) What is the freezing point of water? _____ (1)

(b) Explain why it would not be a good idea to leave a garden hose full of water during the winter.

_____ (2)

6 Two identical cloths are dipped in water and hung in different places to dry.

(a) Suggest two factors that might affect the rate at which the cloths dry.

_____ (2)

(b) What has happened to the water from the cloths once they are dry?

_____ (2)

B: Solutions

This topic is about what happens when materials are mixed with water. You need to know about soluble and insoluble materials and the factors affecting how quickly materials dissolve.

Mixing with water

When materials are mixed with water, some **dissolve** (seem to disappear) and some do not.

- Substances that dissolve are **soluble** (e.g. salt, sugar).
- Substances that do not dissolve are **insoluble** (e.g. sand, chalk).
- Insoluble materials made from tiny particles float in the water and make a cloudy mixture called a **suspension**.

> dissolve   soluble
> insoluble   suspension

Solutions

When a soluble substance dissolves in water or another liquid, the mixture is called a **solution**.

A solution has two parts:

- the dissolved solid is called the **solute**
- the liquid is called the **solvent**.

> solute
> solution
> solvent

> To remember which is which it helps to learn the sentence <u>The SOLUte is the SOLUble solid</u>.

Factors affecting the rate of dissolving

There are three key variables (factors) that affect how quickly a substance will dissolve:

- The temperature of the solvent.
- The size of the particles of the solute.
- The amount of stirring.

You may have carried out a fair test experiment to test the effect of these variables.

For example how does the temperature of the water affect the time taken for sugar to dissolve?

In this experiment:

- the independent variable is the temperature of the water
- the dependent variable is the time taken for the sugar to dissolve
- the control variables are the volume of water, the mass of sugar, the crystal size of sugar and the amount of stirring.

When we investigate the factors affecting how quickly a substance dissolves, we find the following patterns:

- The warmer the solvent, the quicker the solute dissolves.
- The smaller the crystals of solute, the quicker they dissolve.
- The more the mixture is stirred, the quicker the solute dissolves.

> ### Exam tip
> You might be asked to draw and/or interpret a bar chart or line graph showing data from dissolving experiments. Use the skills from Chapter 1 to help you to do this.

Conservation of mass

When materials dissolve they do not disappear or change into anything new. They break up into tiny pieces, too small to see, and mix with the solvent.

The mass of the solution is equal to the mass of the solvent plus the mass of the solute. For example, if 100 g of water and 20 g of sugar are mixed together, the mass of the sugar solution will be 120 g.

Try

1 Imogen dissolves some crystals of copper sulfate in water to make a blue solution. In this solution what is

(a) the solute _____ (1)

(b) the solvent _____ (1)

2 Fill in the gaps in the following sentences.

Two substances are mixed with water. Substance A dissolves to form a clear solution so it is _____ . Substance B forms a cloudy mixture and does not dissolve so it is _____ . (2)

Test

Test time: 08:00

3 Some children carry out a test to find out how the size of sugar crystals affects the time taken to dissolve. They have three different sizes of crystals. They add some of each size to water in a beaker and stir. They measure the time taken for the crystals to dissolve.

(a) What is the dependent variable in this experiment?

_____ (1)

(b) Suggest three ways in which the children can make this a fair test.

_____

_____ (3)

4 The results of an experiment are shown in the table.

Speed of stirring	Time taken for crystals to dissolve, in minutes			
	1st test	2nd test	3rd test	Mean
Slow	6.0	5.4	5.1	5.5
Medium	2.5	3.5		3.0
Fast	1.3	1.7	1.5	

(a) Fill in the gaps in the table. (2)

(b) Draw a bar chart on separate graph paper to show the mean results. (3)

(c) What pattern is shown by these results?

_____ (2)

C: Separating mixtures

A mixture is two or more materials mixed together but not chemically joined. The different parts of a mixture can therefore be separated.

You need to be able to say which separation technique is appropriate to use in different situations and to be able to draw scientific diagrams to show the apparatus used.

Separation techniques

The important techniques that you need to know about for your 11+ exam are:

- sieving
- decanting
- filtration
- evaporation.

> Look out for mixtures containing iron filings. Since iron is the only common magnetic metal (see topic D) you can remove the iron filings using a magnet.

Sieving

A sieve is used to separate a mixture of dry materials of different sizes, e.g. gravel and sand.

The smaller particles will pass through the sieve and the larger ones will be left behind in the sieve. Sieving is also used to separate the different parts of soils (see topic G).

Decanting

Decanting is used to separate an insoluble solid from a liquid, when the solid sinks to the bottom of the container, e.g. sand and water.

The mixture is left to settle. The liquid is then very carefully poured off, leaving the solid behind in the container.

Filtration

Filtration is used to separate an insoluble solid from a suspension, when the solid does not easily settle to the bottom of the container, for example chalk and water.

filtrate
residue

A piece of filter paper is folded and placed in a filter funnel. The mixture is poured through.

The liquid passes through the tiny holes in the filter paper. This is the **filtrate**.

The insoluble solid stays behind in the filter. This is the **residue**.

The apparatus for filtering is drawn like this:

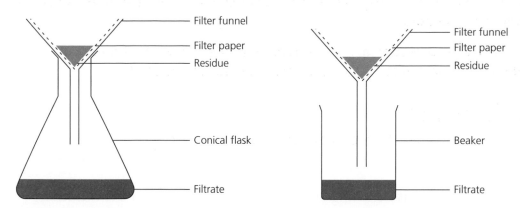

When drawing science diagrams, always draw with a sharp pencil and use a ruler for all straight lines. Make sure your diagram is neat and remember to label it.

Evaporation

Evaporation is used to obtain the solute from a solution, for example salt from salt solution or sea water.

The solvent is heated to evaporate the solvent. The solute is left in the container (usually an evaporating basin).

The apparatus used to evaporate a solution is drawn like this:

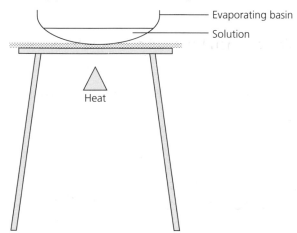

Do not heat the solution until it is completely dry as hot crystals will begin to spit out of the evaporating basin.

Solutions can be left to evaporate slowly in a warm place such as a sunny windowsill. This method makes the solute form bigger crystals.

Remember that solutions cannot be separated by filtration because the particles of the dissolved solute are small enough to pass through the filter paper.

Sometimes more than one separation technique is needed to separate a mixture fully. Think about the properties of the items in the mixture, e.g. a mixture of sand and salt. Sand is insoluble but salt is soluble.

To separate this mixture:

1 Add water to the mixture and stir to dissolve the salt.
2 Filter the mixture.
3 Evaporate the water from the salt solution to obtain the salt.

Train

1 On a separate sheet of paper, practise drawing and labelling the diagrams of the filtration and evaporation apparatus until you can draw them from memory.
   Remember to use a sharp pencil and a ruler.

Try

2 What separation technique would you use to separate the following mixtures?
   (a) gravel and water _____ (1)
   (b) dried pasta and salt _____ (1)
   (c) iron filings and sand _____ (1)
3 After filtration, what name is given to
   (a) the material left in the filter paper _____ (1)
   (b) the liquid that passes through the filter paper? _____ (1)

Test

Test time: 08:00

4 Some children want to find out how much salt there is in sea water.
   They weigh a sample of sea water and then heat it to evaporate the water.

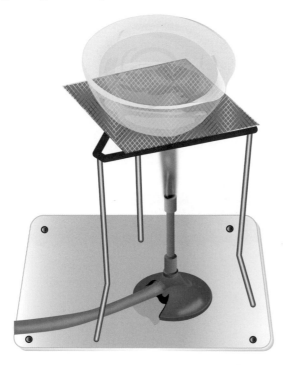

(a) Suggest two safety precautions that the children should take.

1 _____ (1)

2 _____ (1)

(b) Why can filtration not be used to separate a mixture of salt and water?

_____

_____ (2)

(c) The sample of sea water weighed 100 g. The children found that they had 3.5 g of dry salts at the end. Calculate the mass of the water in the sample. Show your working.

_____

_____

_____ (2)

5 Describe how you could separate a mixture of salt, sand and wood chips.

_____

_____

_____

_____ (4)

D: Chemical changes 1: Burning and rusting

Chemical changes are those that result in the formation of new materials. You need to know about rusting and burning as examples of chemical change. You need to be aware that most materials are made by chemical changes, either natural or man-made.

Chemical changes all around us

Most of the changes we observe in the world around us are chemical ones.

Some chemical changes occur naturally, for example fruit ripening, digestion of food, photosynthesis.

Some chemical changes occur due to man-made (synthetic) processes, for example superglue setting, making concrete, food cooking, plaster of Paris setting, making materials such as plastic.

> To decide whether a change is physical or chemical, think about whether it would be possible to change it back to the starting material(s). Physical changes are reversible. Chemical changes are usually non-reversible.

Important chemical changes

Burning

Chemical changes often release energy and in some cases we can make that energy useful.

Materials that are burnt to release energy are called **fuels**. Examples include: wood, coal, oil, gas and candle wax.

Coal, oil and gas are called **fossil fuels** because they were formed from the remains of dead plants and animals millions of years ago.

We burn fuels in burning reactions to release energy to make electricity and for heating and cooking. In a candle the useful energy released is light.

Burning needs a supply of oxygen from the air. You may have seen an experiment to show this when a candle is covered with an upturned jam jar. After a while the candle goes out because there is not enough oxygen left to keep it burning.

The new materials formed when fuels are burnt are gases (carbon dioxide gas and water vapour).

Burning is a non-reversible reaction. Once a fuel has been burnt we cannot turn the carbon dioxide gas and water vapour back into the fuel.

> fossil fuel
> fuel

Rusting

Some chemical changes are not helpful. Rusting makes iron and steel weaker. In certain situations, for example when steel is used to make bridges, this can be dangerous.

Iron reacts with air (oxygen) to form a crumbly brown material known as rust. Iron is the only metal that forms rust. Steel rusts because it contains iron.

The nails only rusted in the control test tube where they were exposed to both air (oxygen) and water.

Rusting is a non-reversible change. To prevent iron and steel from rusting it is necessary to stop oxygen and water from coming into contact with the surface of the metal.

This can be done by:

● painting the surface
● covering the surface with oil
● covering the surface with a layer of plastic
● **galvanising** the surface.

Galvanising means to cover the surface in a thin layer of another metal, usually zinc.

galvanising

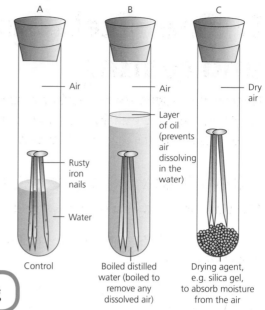

A   B   C

— Air   — Air   — Dry air

— Layer of oil (prevents air dissolving in the water)

— Rusty iron nails

— Water

Control

Boiled distilled water (boiled to remove any dissolved air)

Drying agent, e.g. silica gel, to absorb moisture from the air

Try

1 For each of the changes below, state whether it is **reversible** or **non-reversible**.

(a) cooking an egg ⎯⎯⎯⎯⎯ (1)   (b) an ice lolly melting ⎯⎯⎯⎯⎯ (1)

(c) a banana ripening ⎯⎯⎯⎯⎯ (1)   (d) a pond freezing ⎯⎯⎯⎯⎯ (1)

(e) toast burning ⎯⎯⎯⎯⎯ (1)

2 What is a fuel?

⎯⎯⎯⎯⎯⎯⎯⎯⎯⎯⎯⎯⎯⎯⎯⎯⎯⎯⎯⎯⎯ (1)

Test

Test time: 08:00

3 (a) State two conditions that must be present for iron or steel to rust.

⎯⎯⎯⎯⎯⎯⎯⎯⎯⎯⎯⎯⎯⎯⎯⎯⎯⎯⎯⎯⎯ (2)

(b) Sally's father says that his car rusts more quickly in the winter when there is salt on the road. Describe how Sally could find out if iron rusts more quickly in salty water than in ordinary tap water.

⎯⎯⎯⎯⎯⎯⎯⎯⎯⎯⎯⎯⎯⎯⎯⎯⎯⎯⎯⎯⎯

⎯⎯⎯⎯⎯⎯⎯⎯⎯⎯⎯⎯⎯⎯⎯⎯⎯⎯⎯⎯⎯

⎯⎯⎯⎯⎯⎯⎯⎯⎯⎯⎯⎯⎯⎯⎯⎯⎯⎯⎯⎯⎯

⎯⎯⎯⎯⎯⎯⎯⎯⎯⎯⎯⎯⎯⎯⎯⎯⎯⎯⎯⎯⎯ (4)

(c) Cars are coated with several layers of paint. How does this help to stop them rusting?

⎯⎯⎯⎯⎯⎯⎯⎯⎯⎯⎯⎯⎯⎯⎯⎯⎯⎯⎯⎯⎯ (1)

4 (a) What is a fossil fuel?

⎯⎯⎯⎯⎯⎯⎯⎯⎯⎯⎯⎯⎯⎯⎯⎯⎯⎯⎯⎯⎯ (2)

(b) Name a solid fossil fuel. ⎯⎯⎯⎯⎯⎯⎯⎯⎯⎯⎯⎯⎯ (1)

E: Chemical changes 2: New materials and indicators

Chemical reactions may be naturally-occurring or man-made. All chemical reactions result in the formation of new materials, some of which may be useful to us in a variety of ways. You need to be able to recognise the difference between natural and man-made (synthetic) materials.

Making new materials

Nearly all materials are made through chemical reactions.

Naturally-occurring chemical reactions in the cells of living things make new materials for them to grow and reproduce. Sometimes this creates materials that are useful for humans as well, for example wood, cotton, wool.

> chemist
> man-made
> naturally-occuring
> synthetic

Many materials used to make everyday things are created by **man-made (synthetic)** processes. For example, plastics, paraffin wax, concrete.

Chemists use chemical changes to make new materials that are useful. For example, Spencer Silver was working with chemical changes to make stronger glues for the space industry. While he was doing this he discovered the special 'tacky' glue used for sticky notes when an experiment did not turn out the way he expected.

Ruth Berenito was an American chemist who saw that cotton fabrics were hard to care for because they became so crumpled and hard to iron when washed. She carried out experiments to find a way of coating the fibres of cotton fabric to stop them becoming so bent and tangled when they were put into water.

Indicators

All solutions can be described as being **acidic**, **neutral** or **alkaline**.

> acidic   indicator
> alkaline   neutral
> extract

- Acidic: lemon juice, vinegar.
- Neutral: salt solution, sugar solution, pure water.
- Alkaline: bicarbonate of soda solution, many cleaning products.

Safe acids taste sour. Safe alkalis may taste or feel soapy. Neutral substances are neither acidic nor alkaline.

Many acids and alkalis are not safe to taste or handle so we use **indicators** to tell us whether a solution is acidic, neutral or alkaline.

Indicators are substances, often extracted from natural materials, which react with acids and alkalis to give diagnostic colour changes.

Litmus is *pink* in acidic solutions, *blue* in alkaline solutions and *purple* in neutral solutions.

Litmus may be in the form of a solution or as test papers.

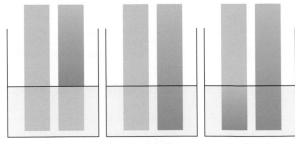

Beaker A:
If both strips show pink, the solution is acidic.

Beaker B:
If the pink strip stays pink and the blue strip stays blue, the solution is neutral.

Beaker C:
If both strips show blue, the solution is alkaline.

The test papers will usually be either pink or blue. It is good practice to use one of each when testing a solution to make sure that you get the right answer.

Another naturally-occurring indicator can be extracted from red cabbage:

- Chop the leaves finely.
- Add water.
- Boil until the water becomes strongly coloured.
- Filter the mixture.

Red cabbage extract is *red* in acidic solutions, *purple* in neutral solutions and *green* in alkaline solutions.

Try

1 Underline the word that best completes the following sentences.

   (a) An example of a naturally-occurring material is

      A glass   B paraffin wax   C plastic   D wood

   (b) An example of a synthetic material is

      A beeswax   B clay   C concrete   D wool   (2)

2 What colour is shown by litmus solution when it is added to lemon juice? Explain your answer.

_____ (2)

Test

Test time: 09:00

3 Complete the table, showing whether each material is natural or man-made and suggesting two uses for each, based on your knowledge of their properties.

Material	Natural or man-made	Might be used for
Plastic		
	Man-made	Windows, spectacles
Clay		
Wood		

(5)

4 Chemists are working hard to find plant-based materials as alternatives to oil products for making plastics. Suggest one reason why this is necessary.

_____ (1)

5 (a) Describe how you might extract the coloured pigment from some orange berries.

   _____

   _____

   _____ (4)

   (b) It is found that the orange berry extract shows orange in acids, dark yellow in neutral liquids and paler yellow in alkalis. Would you consider this to be a good indicator? Explain your answer.

   _____

   _____ (2)

F: Rocks

There are many different types of rock making up the Earth. We can tell them apart by looking carefully at their appearance and physical properties, such as hardness and texture. You should be able to describe how sedimentary rocks form and how the remains of living things become fossilised.

Types of rock

Rocks are made up either from **crystals** of minerals or from **grains** of sand, silt or tiny shells.

crystal
fossil
grain
igneous rock
impermeable
permeable
sediment
sedimentary rock

Rocks made from crystals

Rocks made of crystals (for example granite) were formed when hot, molten rock from deep inside the Earth came near to the surface or out of a volcano and then cooled. These rocks are called **igneous rocks**.

Rocks made of crystals are:

● hard and cannot be scratched easily
● mostly **impermeable** (water cannot drain through them).

Rocks made from grains

Rocks made from grains are called **sedimentary rocks**.

Some (for example sandstone) were made when sand and silt were carried to the sea by rivers. They settled to the bottom of the sea in layers called **sediments**. As more and more layers built up, the ones lower down bacome squeezed and turned into rock.

Some sedimentary rocks (limestone and chalk) were made from the shells of billions of tiny sea creatures that sank to the bottom of the ocean when the animals died.

Sedimentary rocks are:

● softer than crystal rocks and can be scratched more easily
● **permeable**
● built up in layers, often of different colours.

Fossils

Fossils are made from the remains of living things that died millions of years ago.

The remains fell into a lake or ocean and became covered by sediment.

As layers of sediment built up the plant and animal remains were squeezed with the layers of sediment and turned into rock.

Usually it is only the hard parts of an organism that become fossilised but very occasionally fossils are found with traces of soft parts such as skin or feathers.

Sometimes the remains of an animal make an imprint in the sediment but then decay or are swept away by sea currents. The imprint then becomes filled with the next layer of sediment and the shape of the organism is all that remains in the rock.

Try

1 Use words from the box to fill in the gaps in the following sentences. Each word may be used once, more than once or not at all.

| crystals | granite | limestone | sandstone | sedimentary |

Rocks made up from _____ were formed when molten rock from deep inside the Earth cooled.

Rocks made from layers of silt, sand or shells of sea creatures are called _____ rocks. _____ is a rock made from layers of sand. _____ is made from the shells of tiny sea creatures.

Fossils are found in _____ rocks. (5)

2 Rock A is a white rock that can be scratched easily. Rock B is a grey rock that is very hard and cannot be scratched easily.

Which rock, A or B, is more likely to be made up from crystals? _____ (1)

Test

Test time: 06:00

3 Describe two differences between the properties of sedimentary rocks and the properties of igneous rocks.

_____

_____

_____

_____ (4)

4 Archaeopteryx was a bird-like creature that lived millions of years ago. It was first discovered as a fossil in Germany in 1861. The fossil showed the bones and feathers of the creature clearly.

(a) What was unusual about this fossil?

_____ (1)

(b) Describe briefly how the fossil of Archaeopteryx would have formed.

_____

_____

_____ (3)

G: Soils

Soil is an important part of the environment. You need to know about the characteristics of some different types of soil. You also need to be able to describe how to separate soil particles of different sizes and how to compare the permeability of different soils.

What is soil?

Soil has four important parts:

- Particles of weathered rock.
- Remains of living things.
- Air spaces (plant roots and other organisms need air).
- Water.

Soils differ in several ways, including:

- the sizes of the rocky particles.
- the amount of once-living material (**humus**) in the soil.

humus
permeability

Humus

Humus is the name given to the remains of living things that are mixed into the soil. When plants and animals die, their remains are broken down and taken into the soil by bacteria, fungi and animals such as worms.

Humus has two important functions:

- It contains mineral salts that enrich the soil and help plants to grow well.
- It helps to hold water in the soil so that plants can take it up into their roots.

Separating soil particles

Particles in soil samples can be separated according to their size in two ways.

1 Dry samples can be separated using a set of soil sieves. Each layer keeps back a different size of particles, largest at the top and smallest at the bottom.
2 A sample of soil and water can be placed in a jar with a screw lid. The jar is shaken. The largest particles settle to the bottom first and the rest follow in order of size with the smallest at the top.

Particle size and permeability

The **permeability** of a soil is the rate at which water drains through it.

This can be tested by placing a sample in a funnel over a measuring cylinder.

Water is poured in. The permeability is measured by seeing what volume of water has drained through in a given time (for example one minute).

The larger the particles, the quicker water drains through.

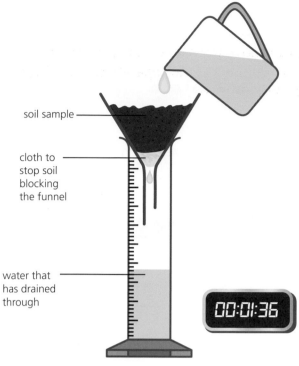

soil sample

cloth to stop soil blocking the funnel

water that has drained through

00:01:36

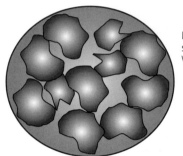

Large particles have big spaces between them. Water drains through easily.

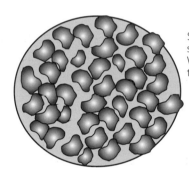

Small particles have small spaces between them. Water cannot drain through easily.

Soil types

There are three main soil types with different properties.

Sand – mostly large particles, drains fast, plants may suffer from lack of water.

Clay – mostly very small particles, drains very slowly, air spaces may become flooded. Clay soils can be moulded into different shapes.

clay
loam
sand

Loam – soil with an even mixture of different sized particles and plenty of humus, water drains well but some is held by the humus.

Loam is the best type of soil for plants to grow in.

Try

1 (a) What is humus?

_____

_____

_____ (2)

(b) Give two benefits of having humus in a soil.

1 _____

2 _____ (2)

2 Name three different types of soil.

_____ (3)

3 Some children were investigating soils.

They took dry samples of soil and separated the particles using sieves. Each sample weighed 25 g.

Here are their results.

Soil	Mass of large particles, in g	Mass of medium particles, in g	Mass of small particles, in g
A	15		2
B	3	6	16
C	8	7	10

(a) Complete the table by calculating the missing value. (1)

(b) Complete the bar chart below by drawing bars to show the mass of large, medium and small particles for Soil A. (3)

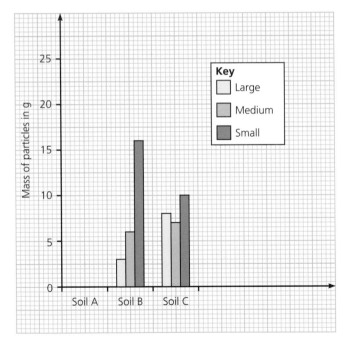

(c) Which soil, A, B or C, is

(i) loam _____ (1)

(ii) clay soil? _____ (1)

(d) Which soil would have the quickest drainage rate? Explain your answer.

_____

_____

_____ (3)

4 Some children compared the permeabilities of two soils.

They put a scoop of each soil into a funnel, set in a beaker.

They poured water in both funnels and left them for one minute.

They compared the volume of water in the beakers.

(a) How would their results tell them which soil was the most permeable?

_____ (1)

(b) Suggest two ways in which they might have improved their investigation.

1 _____

2 _____ (2)

(c) Impermeable soils often contain very few earthworms. Suggest a reason for this.

_____

_____ (2)

Test 2 Chemistry

1 Underline the word or phrase that best completes the following sentences.

(a) An example of a synthetic material is

| A | cotton | B | polythene |
| C | timber | D | wool |

(b) Different sized particles in a sample of dry soil are best separated by

| A | decanting | B | filtering |
| C | sieving | D | washing |

(c) The change of state from a vapour to a liquid is called

| A | condensation | B | evaporation |
| C | freezing | D | melting |

(d) Feathers are good thermal insulators because they

| A | are a natural material | B | come from birds |
| C | feel light | D | trap air | (4) |

2 (a) Farm gates made from steel are often galvanised to stop them rusting. Explain what is meant by the term 'galvanising' and how the process protects the gate.

_____

_____ (2)

(b) The frame of a bicycle is protected from rust with paint. The chain is protected with oil. Suggest why oil is better than paint to protect the chain.

_____

_____ (2)

3 Sara was investigating some water from a river.

(a) There were lots of tiny pieces of plant material floating in the water. In the space draw a labelled diagram of the apparatus Sara should use to remove the plant material from the water.

(4)

(b) Sara wanted to find out if there were any materials dissolved in the river water. What method could she use to find out?

_____

_____ (2)

4 (a) Name the measuring device used to find the temperature of an object.

_____ (1)

(b) What is meant by the term 'freezing point'?

_____ (1)

(c) What is the boiling point of water?

_____ (1)

5 Some children were investigating burning.

They weighed a candle and then lit it.

They let it burn for 30 minutes and then carefully put out the flame.

They weighed it again.

(a) Fill in the gaps in the following sentences.

Burning is a _____ change. The wax of the candle is
the _____ . For burning to take place oxygen from the
_____ is also needed.   (3)

(b) How would you expect the mass of the candle to change in this experiment?
Explain your answer.

_____

_____ (3)

6 Fill in the gaps in the table about testing liquids with litmus.

Liquid	Colour of pink litmus paper	Colour of blue litmus paper	Acidic, alkaline or neutral?
A	pink	pink	
B		blue	alkaline
C			neutral

(4)

7 Here is a key that can be used to identify rocks. Look at it carefully and then answer the
questions.

(a) Which rock is hard and made up from crystals that are large? _____ (1)

(b) What is the difference between sandstone and shale?

_____ (1)

(c) Use the information in the key to show the features of slate.

_____

_____ (3)

Record your score and time here and at the start of the book.

Score ☐ / 32 Time ☐ : ☐

④ Physics: Forces, light, sound, electricity and space

What is physics?

Physics is the study of how things work. In your physics lessons you will have learnt about different types of forces and the ways in which forces affect the movement of objects. You will have studied how sound and light help us to make sense of the world around us and communicate with each other. You will have probably done experiments to explore shadows and reflections and learnt about how to take care of your ears and eyes.

In physics you will also have learnt about how to make simple electric circuits, the effect of changing the components in the circuit and how to use electricity safely. Finally you will have had the opportunity to learn about space, especially the solar system to which planet Earth belongs.

You have been experiencing how things work ever since you were a very tiny baby. When you are answering questions in physics, it often helps if you stop and think about your own experience and imagine what you would see, hear or feel in the situation in the question. These 'thought experiments' give you an opportunity to sort your ideas out and present them in a concise and clear way.

In the exam you may be asked to describe particular physics experiments or to work with data from an investigation. Make sure that you read the question carefully to make sure that you understand what you are being asked to do. Sometimes you will need to do some simple calculations. You may use a calculator but remember to check that your answer is reasonable and redo the calculation if it seems to be wrong. If you are asked to draw a circuit diagram, remember to use a sharp pencil and a ruler.

Advice to parents

The study of physics at this level draws strongly on experience. Physics lessons are an opportunity to think about the phenomena that are part of everyday life and to think about what causes them to happen.

The key to success in answering physics questions in the exam is to enhance these links to your child's experience and to focus on working things out rather than giving set answers from memory. This can be supported by making a point of wondering why or how things happen on a day-to-day basis and encouraging the application of the concepts studied in class to as many real-life situations as possible. It is also helpful to encourage your child to explain ideas and observations clearly and concisely, using scientific vocabulary as much as possible, so that they develop the language needed to answer exam questions.

Setting the scene: Types of force

Forces are pushes and pulls. A push and a pull can sometimes work together to make a turning effect. Pushes and pulls affect the way in which objects move. They can also change the shape of objects. You need to be able to recognise the different types of force and to be able to say what effect they have on the object upon which they are acting.

Types of force

There are nine different types of force that you have learnt about.

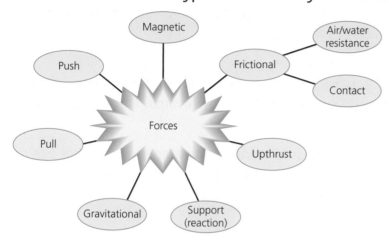

1   A mnemonic is a way of remembering lists. It is a sentence in which each word starts with the starting letter of one of the items in the list. Make up a mnemonic to help you to remember the nine types of force.

Forces acting on objects

When forces act on an object they may have a variety of effects.

- They may start the object moving.
- They may stop a moving object.
- They may make a moving object speed up or slow down.
- They may change the shape of an object.

To have an effect most forces have to be actually in contact with the object. For example you would not make a football start to move until your foot touches it.

An exception to this rule is magnetic forces, which can act at a distance. (See topic D.)

2   Think about things that you do each day. See if you can find examples of things that have each of the four effects in the list. Try to say what type of force you used.

   For example, when you opened this book you made a pulling force that made the pages of the book start to move.

A: More about forces

Sometimes forces happen automatically in response to another force. You need to know about these reaction forces. You also need to know about how to measure forces and how forces can be represented in diagrams.

Reaction forces

When you pull on a spring or an elastic band you can feel a force pulling back in the opposite direction. If you push down on the table, you can feel the table pushing back up. We call these forces **reaction** forces. Sometimes, as in these examples, reaction forces are easy to feel. Sometimes they are hidden.

> reaction
> support force
> upthrust

If you are sitting on a chair the gravitational force is pulling you down towards the centre of the Earth. There must be an upwards force stopping you from sinking downwards. This is called the **support force**.

Another reaction force is **upthrust**. This is the upward support force, created in water, that allows things to float.

Measuring forces

Forces are measured using a force meter, sometimes called a newton spring balance. The unit of force is the newton (N).

You may have used force meters with different ranges, for example 0–10 N or 0–25 N. Each force meter has a spring inside. The size of the force that can be measured depends on the amount of reaction force that the spring can make when pulled or squeezed.

Showing forces on diagrams

When drawing forces diagrams we use arrows to show the direction in which a force is acting.

For example, this diagram represents the forces acting on a motor boat.

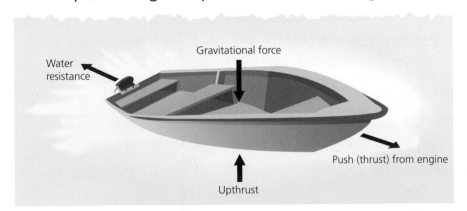

Water resistance

Gravitational force

Push (thrust) from engine

Upthrust

> Always draw in pencil and use a ruler to draw the arrows neatly and clearly.

Try

1 What is the unit of force? _____ (1)

2 (a) What is the name of the force that is pulling you towards the centre of the Earth?

_____ (1)

(b) What force is stopping you from sinking through the chair you are sitting on?

_____ (1)

Test

Test time: 07:00

3 The diagram shows a car moving along the road. Add labelled arrows to the diagram to show the following forces acting on the car: *push from the engine, gravitational force, support force, air resistance.*

(4)

4 Give the size of the force shown on each of the force meter scales.

(a)

(b)

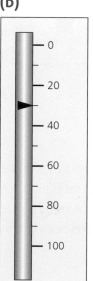

(c)

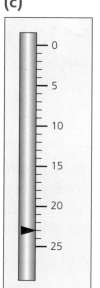

_____ _____ _____

(3)

5 Using your knowledge of forces, explain why a boat floats on water.

_____

_____ (2)

B: Mechanisms

We use forces to do jobs. Sometimes the force required is too great for the job to be done by hand. Mechanisms are devices that people have invented to make jobs possible. You need to know about the various types of mechanism and how they help us to do jobs more easily.

What is a mechanism?

Mechanisms are devices that make jobs easier. When we try to move something we apply a force, called the **effort**. A mechanism increases the effect of this effort.

Types of mechanism

There are three types of mechanism that you need to know about:

● levers   ● gears   ● pulleys.

Levers

Levers are sometimes described as force magnifiers.

A lever consists of a rigid bar or rod that turns round a fixed point called the pivot or fulcrum.

Here is a diagram of a simple lever being used.

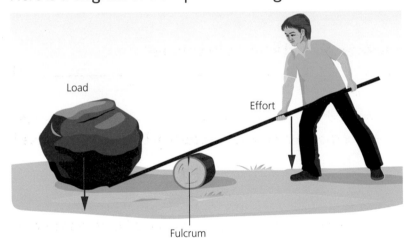

The lever allows the man to lift the heavy load. The fulcrum is placed near the load. The man applies the effort force as far from the fulcrum as possible. The further away from the fulcrum, the more effect the effort has.

Many everyday tools, such as spanners, scissors and wheelbarrows, are levers. A see-saw is also a lever.

Gears

Gears are usually wheels with teeth, called cogs, around the outside. They are found in places where we want to change the effect of a force that makes a rotation. Gears are found in engines, on bicycles and in clocks as well as in many items of heavy machinery. The turning movement is transferred from one gear to another, either by interlocking the cogs or using a chain.

Here is an example of gears being used on a bicycle.

The gear wheel on the pedals has more teeth than the one on the back wheel of the bicycle. One turn of the pedals makes the back wheel turn several times. This allows a cyclist to travel faster.

Pulleys

A pulley consists of a wheel and a rope. The rope passes over the wheel. The load is attached at one end of the rope and the effort is applied at the other end. This changes the direction in which the effort force is applied.

Two or more pulleys can be linked together to allow the load to be lifted with a smaller effort.

Try

1 (a) What is the name given to the fixed point around which a lever turns?

_____ (1)

(b) Name two everyday devices that use levers.

_____ (2)

2 Use words from the box to fill in the gaps in the following sentences. Each word may be used once, more than once or not at all.

downward	gear	larger	pulley	smaller	upward

A simple _____ is a wheel with a rope running over it. To lift a load the effort force is applied in a _____ direction. Two or more of the wheels linked together allows a _____ force to be used to lift the load.   (3)

Test   Test time: 03:00

3 The diagram shows a spanner being used to turn a nut. Add an arrow to the diagram to show how the effort force should be applied to turn the nut in a clockwise direction most easily.

(2)

4 A cyclist changes the gears on her bicycle so that the gear wheel on the pedals has three times as many cogs as the one on the back wheel. She turns the pedal wheel once. What will happen to the back wheel of her bicycle?

_____ (2)

C: Friction and air resistance

Friction is an important force that is sometimes useful and sometimes a nuisance. You need to know how friction is caused and how it affects the motion of objects.

Friction and air resistance

Friction is a force that is created when two surfaces rub against one another.

Contact friction is caused when two solid surfaces move past each other. Rough surfaces cause more friction than smooth ones.

Friction works in the opposite direction to the movement of the object.

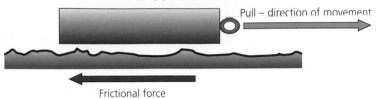

Pull – direction of movement

Frictional force

Air resistance is the frictional force between a moving object and the air.

A similar frictional force is created when objects move through water.

Effects of friction

- Friction causes moving objects to slow down.
- Friction may stop an object from moving.
- Friction can cause the rubbing surfaces to wear out and become hot.

You may have done some experiments comparing the frictional force created by different surfaces. For example, measuring how far a car travels across different surfaces.

Helpful or a nuisance?

Examples of helpful friction

- Friction between your shoes and the floor stops you from slipping over.
- Friction between a vehicle's tyres and the road stops the vehicle from skidding.
- Friction between a car's brakes and the wheels slows or stops the car.

Examples of unhelpful friction

- Air resistance and friction between tyres and the road slow vehicles down.
- Friction between the moving parts of machinery makes it harder for them to move and makes them wear out and get hot.

Working with friction

We can increase friction by making surfaces rougher, for example the **tread** on car tyres, adding grit to icy roads.

streamlining
tread

We can decrease friction by making it easier for surfaces to move past each other, for example by adding oil or by rubbing the surfaces smooth.

We can decrease air and water resistance by **streamlining** (making the moving vehicle or object in a smooth sleek shape that allows air or water to flow past it easily).

Friction and road safety

Friction affects how quickly a car can stop in an emergency. The distance travelled between when the brakes are applied and the car coming to a rest is called the **stopping distance**. Stopping distances are set out for drivers in the **Highway Code**.

- The faster the car is travelling, the bigger the frictional force needed to stop the car, so the longer the stopping distance.
- Wet or icy conditions decrease friction and increase stopping distances.

Highway Code stopping distance

Try

1 (a) How is friction caused?

_____ (1)

(b) What is meant by the term 'air resistance'?

_____ (1)

2 Mrs Lomas's front door hinge was stiff. She put some oil on it. Explain how the oil makes the hinge move more easily.

_____

_____ (2)

Test

Test time: 10:00

3 The table shows the stopping distances for a range of different speeds (1 car length = 4 m).

Speed of vehicle in miles per hour	Total stopping distance, in car lengths
20	3
30	6
40	9
50	
60	18
70	24

(a) On a separate sheet of graph paper plot these points on a graph with Speed of vehicle on the horizontal axis and Total stopping distance on the vertical axis. (5)

(b) Draw a smooth curve between the points. (1)

(c) Use your graph to estimate the stopping distance at 50 miles per hour and fill your answer into the table. Show your working on the graph. (2)

(d) Draw a second line showing what the stopping distances might be if the road was icy. (2)

4 Eloise was investigating how different surfaces affect how far a toy car travelled after running down a ramp.

(a) She used three surfaces: carpet, wood and cardboard. Predict which surface would allow the car to travel the shortest distance. Explain your answer.

_____

_____ (2)

(b) Apart from the friction between the car and the surface, what other force is acting to slow the car down? _____ (1)

D: Magnets

This topic covers magnetic forces, magnetic poles and how a magnet acts as a compass. You also need to know about magnetic and non-magnetic materials and how to carry out experiments to compare the strengths of magnets.

Magnetic poles

All magnets have two **poles** and these are the strongest parts of the magnet.

On bar magnets, the poles are usually at the two ends of the bar.

The poles are called the **north-seeking** and the **south-seeking** poles.

If you hang a magnet from a thread it will always come to rest with the north-seeking pole pointing towards the Earth's north pole.

A **compass** needle is a magnet supported on a pin so it can move freely to line itself with the Earth's magnetic field. The compass can then be used to help with navigation.

> compass
> north-seeking
> pole
> south-seeking

Magnetic forces

All magnets, including the Earth, have an invisible force field around them.

If two magnets come near to each other their force fields will interact with each other.

Two opposite poles (north-seeking and south-seeking) will **attract** (pull) each other.

Two like (same) poles (two north-seeking or two south-seeking) will **repel** (push) each other.

Magnets will attract magnetic materials towards them but they cannot repel anything other than another magnet.

Magnetic effects can pass through some materials, for example the pages of a book or a wooden table top.

> attract
> repel

Magnetic and non-magnetic materials

All non-metals and almost all metals are non-magnetic. Exam questions may ask you to identify which of a group of materials is magnetic.

Iron is the only common magnetic material.

Steel is a mixture of iron and other materials and so it is a magnetic material.

Experiments to compare the strengths of magnets

In the exam you might be asked about how to compare the strengths of magnets. There are several different ways in which this can be done. Some of these use the fact that magnetic forces act over a distance. There are other methods that you might have used and it would be fine to describe these but make sure that your description is really clear.

For example:

1 Place a light magnetic item, such as a paper clip, at the zero on the scale of a ruler. Slowly slide the magnet along the edge of the ruler until the paper clip is attracted to the magnet. Measure the distance over which the clip was attracted.

2 Use a magnet to hold a paper clip through the pages of a book. Count the maximum number of pages the force field will pass through.

Try

1 (a) Where is the force field of a bar magnet strongest, at the middle of the magnet or at the poles?

_____ (1)

(b) Look at the following pairs of magnets. By each pair write whether they will attract or repel each other.

(i) | S   N | | S   N | _____

(ii) | S   N | | N   S | _____   (2)

2 Why does a compass needle always point to the Earth's north pole?

_____ (1)

Test   Test time: 05:00

3 Read the following statements carefully. By each one, say whether the statement is true or false.

(a) A magnet will not attract a plastic toy. _____

(b) A magnet will attract iron filings. _____

(c) A magnet will repel a coin made of copper. _____   (3)

4 A magnet is suspended from a force meter as shown in the diagram.

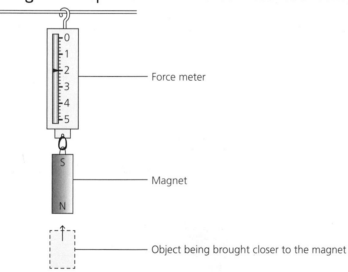

— Force meter

— Magnet

— Object being brought closer to the magnet

A number of objects are brought close to the magnet.

Complete the table by placing a tick in the correct column to show what happens to the reading on the force meter when each object comes towards the magnet.

Object	Change in the force meter reading		
	Increase	Decrease	No change
Steel scissors			
Plastic ruler			
North-seeking pole of a magnet			
South-seeking pole of a magnet			

(4)

E: Light and how we see

Light is a form of energy. We need light to see things. You need to be able to recognise luminous and non-luminous objects. You should be able to describe how light travels and how this allows us to see luminous objects.

Where does light come from?

Light is given out by some objects. We describe these objects as **luminous** sources.

luminous
non-luminous
ray

Examples of luminous objects are: the Sun and other stars, a glowing light bulb, the flame of a candle, the screen of a television set or computer (if it is switched on).

Some objects seem to be luminous but are really just very good at reflecting (bouncing back) light from a luminous source.

Examples of **non-luminous** objects are: the Moon, reflective road signs.

Light travels

Light travels away from the luminous source in straight lines.

Light travels very fast. It is the fastest thing in the Universe.

We show the pathway taken by the light by drawing a straight line. We show the direction in which the light is travelling by adding an arrow to the centre of the straight line. If you are asked to draw a **ray** of light in the exam, remember to use a pencil and a ruler.

The completed ray diagram looks like this:

———————⟶———————

Reflection

mirror
reflect

When light falls on the surface of an object it may be absorbed (taken in), scattered or reflected (bounced back).

Shiny surfaces, such as **mirrors**, **reflect** light so well that we can see a clear image in them.

How we see luminous objects

To see things we use our eyes. We can only see something when light from it enters our eyes.

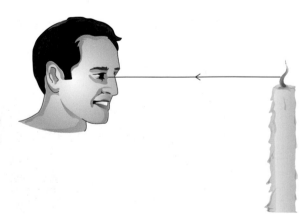

Inside the eye there is a special layer of cells that detect light. Some of these cells detect colours, some detect light and shade. When light falls on these cells they send messages to your brain and your brain interprets these messages to make a picture of the world around you.

We see luminous objects when rays of light coming out of the object enter our eyes.

We can show this on a diagram.

Looking after our eyes

Our eyes are important so we need to look after them. The special light-detecting cells inside our eyes are easily damaged if too much light falls on them.

Direct sunlight is too bright for our eyes so it is a good idea to protect them on a bright day by wearing sunglasses and a cap.

It is not safe to look directly at the Sun, even wearing sunglasses. It is especially dangerous to look at the Sun through a telescope or binoculars as these concentrate the light.

Scientists who study the Sun use special filters to protect their eyes and their cameras and telescopes. If there is an eclipse, people can look at it by using filters made into special sunglasses.

Try

1 Use words from the box to complete the following sentences. Each word may be used once, more than once or not at all.

| filters | luminous | reflected | scattered | shiny | straight | sunglasses |

(a) Light is given out by _____ sources.

(b) Light always travels in _____ lines.

(c) If light bounces off a _____ surface we say that it has been

_____.

(d) Eyes can be protected from sunlight by _____ or

_____.

(4)

2 Give two examples of luminous sources.

_____ (2)

Test

Test time: 05:00

3 When there is a full Moon, a lot of light reaches the surface of the Earth but the Moon is not a luminous source. Explain how this light reaches the Earth.

_____ (2)

4 Monika is watching television. The television screen is a luminous source.

(a) Add to the diagram to show how Monika can see the television.

(2)

(b) Describe briefly how Monika sees the image on the television.

_____

_____ (3)

F: Shadows

Materials may be described as opaque, translucent or transparent, depending on how well light can pass through them. When light falls on an object it may cast a shadow. You need to be able to describe how a shadow is formed and what kinds of materials cast shadows. You also need to know how the size and sharpness of a shadow can be changed.

Light and materials

Materials may be described as **transparent**, **translucent** or **opaque** depending on how easily light can pass through them.

> opaque
> translucent
> transparent

Transparent materials let all light pass through them. We can see through them clearly. Clear glass is transparent so it is a good material for most windows.

Translucent materials let some light through them but it is scattered so that we cannot see clearly through them. Frosted glass is translucent so it is a useful material to make windows for bathrooms.

Opaque materials do not let light pass through. We cannot see through them at all. A wooden door is opaque so you cannot see into a room if the door is closed.

Making shadows

A shadow is an area of darkness caused when an opaque object blocks the light.

The shadow will be the same shape as the opaque object that casts it but the size and sharpness of the shadow can change.

Not included in ISEB 11+ exams

The shape of the shadow is explained by thinking about how the light travels. Light approaches the opaque object in a straight line. When it reaches the object, any light that falls on the object is blocked. Any light that passes the object will carry on in the same straight line. This means that an object-shaped 'hole' is formed in the light making a dark area (shadow) that is the same shape as the object.

Changing shadows

An exam question might ask you about an experiment to investigate how the size and sharpness of a shadow changes as the distances between the light source, the object and the screen change.

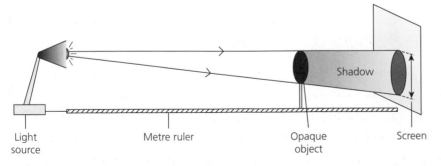

As the object is moved further from the light source and closer to the screen the shadow becomes smaller and sharper.

Try

1 Draw straight lines to join each word to the correct definition.

Words
opaque
transparent
translucent

Definitions
allows some light to pass through
blocks all light
allows all light to pass through

(2)

2 Describe briefly how a shadow is formed.

_____

_____ (2)

Test

Test time: 08:00

3 Some children were investigating shadows. They set up a lamp 50 cm from the wall. They placed an opaque object at different distances from the wall and measured the height of the shadow on the wall. Their results are shown in the table.

Distance between object and wall, in cm	Height of the shadow, in cm
0	5
10	5.8
20	7.7
30	11.0
40	18.4

(a) What pattern is shown in their results?

_____ (2)

The children found it easy to measure the shadow accurately when the object was close to the wall but harder as the distance increased.

(b) Suggest why it became more difficult to measure the shadow accurately as the object was moved further from the wall.

_____ (2)

(c) The teacher suggested that the children should measure the shadow three times at each distance. How might they use this to improve their investigation?

_____ (2)

(d) What was the height of the object? Explain your answer.

_____

_____ (2)

4 Rosie made a shadow puppet. She cut a cat shape out of card. She drew the cat's face and coloured the puppet carefully. She attached a stick and made a cat shadow on the wall.

Give one similarity and one difference between the shadow puppet and the shadow it cast on the wall.

Similarity _____ (1)

Difference _____ (2)

95

G: Reflections

Not included in ISEB 11+ exams

Light is reflected from shiny surfaces in a very predictable way. You need to be able to calculate the path of a reflected ray of light and to draw this accurately on a diagram and describe some applications of mirrors. You need to be able to show how this principle explains how we see non-luminous objects.

The Law of Reflection

The Law of Reflection describes how light is **reflected** from a mirror.

The law applies to reflections from all shiny surfaces but you only need to be able to apply it to reflections from a **plane** (flat) mirror.

The Law of Reflection states that when a ray of light is reflected from a mirror, the **angle of incidence** is equal to the **angle of reflection**.

angle of incidence
angle of reflection
incident
normal
plane
reflected

This diagram shows what this means.

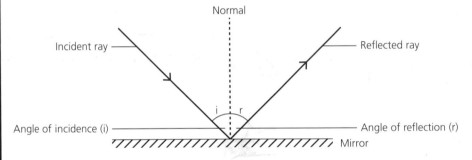

The angle of incidence is the angle between the **incident** ray and the **normal** line (the imaginary line at right angles to the mirror). The angle of reflection is the angle between the reflected ray and the normal line.

In the exam you might be asked to draw or complete a ray diagram like the one just discussed. This must be done accurately so remember to take a protractor to the exam and use a sharp pencil and a ruler when drawing.

Reflection in action

Mirrors are used in many places where people want to see round corners or behind them as well as at home in the bathroom or bedroom.

Examples:

● Mirrors in cars allow drivers to see what is happening behind them.
● Periscopes use two mirrors to allow people to see over or under objects.

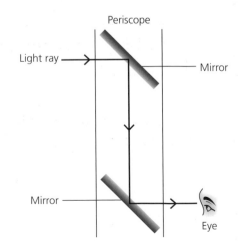

Seeing non-luminous objects

Non-luminous objects do not emit light of their own so we can only see them when light from a luminous source falls onto them and is then reflected into our eyes.

We can show this on a diagram like this.

Light from the Sun (luminous source) falls onto the football (non-luminous object) and is scattered. Some of the reflected light travels into the eyes of the footballer so that he can see it. If there was no light he would not be able to see the ball because no information from it would reach his eyes.

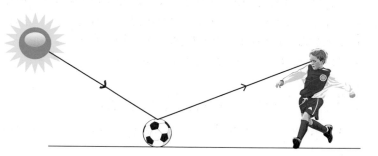

Try

1 Give three everyday uses of mirrors.

_____

_____ (3)

2 Use a protractor to help you to complete the following ray diagrams. In each diagram label the angle of incidence (i) and the angle of reflection (r).

(a) 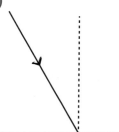   (b)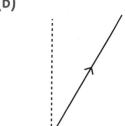

(3)

Test

Test time: 05:00

3 (a) Explain why you cannot read a book when it is completely dark.

_____

_____ (2)

(b) Explain how you can see the book when the light is turned on.

_____

_____ (2)

4 In the space, draw a labelled diagram to show how a mirror might be used to help a motorist to see another car coming round a dangerous corner.

(3)

H: Sound and hearing

Sounds tell us a lot about the world. You need to know about how sounds are made and how they travel. We hear sounds using our ears. You should be able to explain how the ear works to allow us to hear sounds.

How are sounds made?

A sound is a **vibration** (a very rapid backwards and forwards movement). When any object **vibrates** a sound is created.

> vibrate
> vibration

Musical instruments

Musical instruments make sounds in different ways as they cause different things to vibrate.

- In stringed instruments (for example violin, cello, guitar) it is the strings that vibrate.
- In wind instruments air is made to vibrate inside the instrument.
- Percussion instruments (for example drum, triangle) make a sound when they are hit. The whole instrument vibrates.

Making vibrations visible

Sometimes we can see the vibrations but often they are too small, too slow or too fast for our eyes to see. We can sometimes show that something is vibrating even when we cannot see the movement.

- Put a few grains of rice on the skin of a drum and tap the drum gently. You can see how the vibrations of the drum skin make the rice grains jump up and down.
- Strike the prongs of a tuning fork to make it 'sing'. Dip the vibrating prongs into water. You can see how the vibrations make the water splash.

Sounds travel

Sounds can travel, as long as they have something to travel through.

> vacuum

Sounds travel through solids, liquids and gases because they are all made from particles that can vibrate.

Sounds travel fastest through solids, more slowly through liquids and slowest through gases.

Sounds cannot travel through a **vacuum** because there is nothing in a vacuum to vibrate. Space is very nearly a vacuum so sounds do not travel through space.

How we hear

We hear sounds when they enter our ears.

> eardrum
> nerve

Inside the ear there is a thin piece of skin called the **eardrum**. When a sound enters the ear, the eardrum begins to vibrate.

The vibrations are passed through the ear to a coiled structure in the inner ear, which contains lots of tiny hair-like **nerves**.

When these nerves detect the vibrations they pass a message to the brain, which then interprets the message so you are aware of the sound.

Different people have different **hearing ranges**. As people become older the range of sounds that they can hear decreases. Older people often have difficulty hearing higher-pitched sounds.

> deafness
> hearing range

Very loud sounds can damage the eardrum and other parts of the ear. This can cause temporary or permanent **deafness** so it is important to protect your ears from loud noises.

Try

1 Use words from the box to complete the following sentences. Each word may be used once, more than once or not at all.

gases	invisible	solids	particles	vibrate	visible

Sounds are made when objects _____. Sometimes these movements can be seen but often they are _____. Sounds can travel away from the source. Sounds can travel through _____, liquids and _____ because they are made up from _____ that can vibrate. (5)

2 What is vibrating to make the sound in each of the following instruments?

(a) harp _____ (1)

(b) triangle _____ (1)

(c) flute _____ (1)

Test

Test time: 04:00

3 A sailor is on a ship at sea in heavy fog. He cannot see another ship but he hears the sound of its foghorn.

Explain how the sound of the foghorn is heard by the sailor.

_____

_____ (3)

4

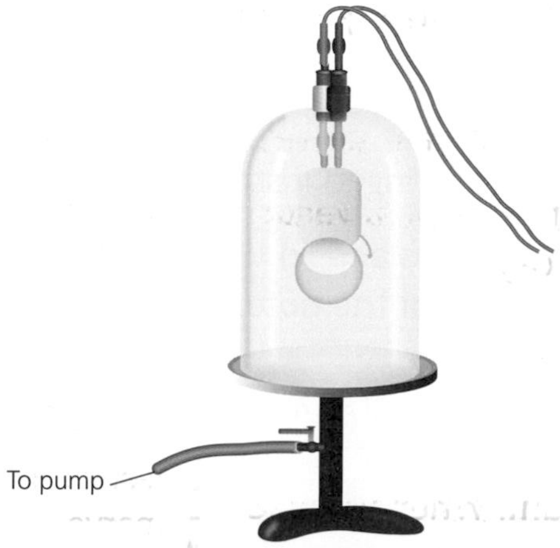

To pump

The picture shows a large jar with a bell inside. The bell is ringing loudly. Ms Matthews uses a pump to suck the air out of the jar. The bell is still ringing.

Suggest what Ms Matthews might hear when she has sucked all the air out of the jar. Explain your answer.

_____

_____ (2)

I: Changing sounds

The sounds we hear throughout the day are all different. Some things can always make the same sound but often the sound can change. You need to be able to identify differences in sounds and explain how they are caused.

Differences between sounds

Sounds can differ in two ways:

pitch
volume

- **Volume** (how loud or quiet a sound is).
- **Pitch** (how high or low the sound is).

Differences in sounds are caused by differences in the vibrations that make the sounds.

- Bigger vibrations make louder sounds; smaller vibrations make quieter sounds.
- Faster vibrations make higher-pitched sounds; slower vibrations make lower-pitched sounds.

Changing volume

To change the volume of the sound we change the energy put in when making the sound to make bigger or smaller vibrations.

- On a stringed instrument we can increase the volume by plucking or bowing the strings more vigorously.
- On a wind instrument we can increase the volume by blowing harder.
- On a percussion instrument we can increase the volume by hitting it harder.

The energy of the sound decreases as the sound passes through the air or other medium. The further away you are from the source of the sound, the quieter it will appear to be.

Changing pitch

The pitch of a sound is changed by speeding up or slowing down the vibrations. Generally a large instrument or object will make a lower-pitched sound than a smaller one.

You need to be able to describe how the pitch of a note can be changed on a stringed instrument such as a violin or guitar.

There are three other factors that affect the pitch of a note in a stringed instrument:

- Thickness of string – the thinner the string, the quicker it vibrates and so the higher the pitch.
- Tightness of string – the tighter the string, the higher the pitch of the note. This can be changed using the pegs on the neck of the instrument.
- Length of string – the shorter the string, the higher the pitch. Players can shorten a string by pressing down on it with a finger.

Try

1 Alex bangs a big drum and then a smaller one.

(a) What difference would there be between the pitch of the smaller drum and that of the larger one?

_____ (2)

(b) Alex's mother asks him to play more quietly. What should Alex do to make the sounds quieter?

_____ (1)

2 Which of the following would **not** change the pitch of a sound? Underline the correct answer.

A Tightening a string

B Plucking a string harder

C Playing a thicker string

D Pushing a finger down on a vibrating string   (1)

Test ● ● ● ● ● ● ● ● ● ● ● ● ● ● ● ● ● ● Test time: 06:00

3 Tuned percussion tubes are hollow plastic tubes that make a sound when they are hit.

Lucia and Robin took the percussion tubes onto the playing field.

Robin banged one of the percussion tubes hard. Lucia listened to the sound as she walked away from Robin.

(a) What change would she notice in the sound as she walked further away?

_____

_____ (2)

Robin said that he thought that the distance the sound travels would depend on the length of the tube.

(b) How would his statement be best described? Tick one box.

- a result ☐
- a prediction ☐
- a conclusion ☐
- an evaluation ☐   (1)

(c) Describe briefly how the children might carry out an investigation to see if Robin is correct.

_____

_____

_____ (3)

4 Idris stretches a thick elastic band and a thin elastic band across an empty tissue box. The elastic bands are both the same length. He makes sounds by plucking the elastic bands.

(a) Which elastic band would you expect to make the lower-pitched note?

_____ (1)

(b) Give one way in which he could make this elastic band make a higher-pitched note.

_____ (1)

J: Making simple circuits

Electricity is a useful form of energy. You need to be able to describe how to connect simple components into a series circuit. You need to know that electricity can only flow through materials that are electrical conductors and how materials can be tested to tell if they conduct electricity. Electricity can be dangerous, so you need to know some basic rules for using electricity safely.

Electric circuits

An electric circuit is a pathway around which electricity can flow.

A circuit needs to have an **electrical** supply. In school experiments this will usually be one or more **cells**.

cell	in series
complete circuit	series circuit
component	terminal

> People often use the term 'battery' to describe a cell. In science a battery is two or more cells joined together. In the exam, make sure that you use these words correctly.

A circuit will also contain one or more devices, such as bulbs, switches, a buzzer or a motor, known as **components**.

The components will only work if they are connected between the **terminals** (connections) of the cells in such a way that a **complete circuit** is made, allowing electricity to flow from one terminal of the cells, through all the components and back to the other terminal of the cells.

A simple circuit where there is just one possible path for the electricity to take is called a **series circuit** and the components are said to be connected **in series**.

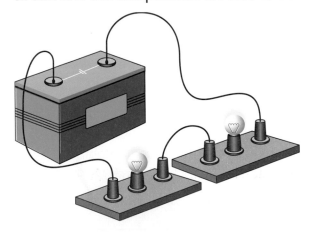

Electrical conductors and insulators

Materials that allow electricity to pass through them are called **electrical conductors**. Materials through which electricity cannot flow are called **electrical insulators**.

| carbon (graphite) |
| electrical conductor |
| electrical insulator |

All metals, for example copper, are electrical conductors. Most non-metals, for example plastic, fabric and wood are electrical insulators.

Carbon (graphite) is an exception. It is a non-metal but is an electrical conductor.

To test a material for electrical conductivity we attach it across a gap in a circuit containing a bulb. If the bulb lights up, the material is a conductor.

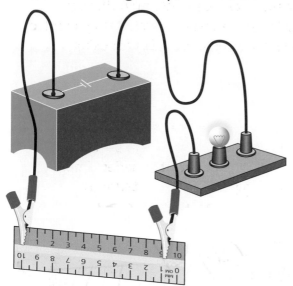

Switches

A switch is a device that opens and closes a gap in a circuit.

The base of the switch is made from plastic, which is an electrical insulator. The other parts of the switch are made from metal that will conduct electricity.

When the switch is open there is a gap between the metal parts. The electricity cannot flow.

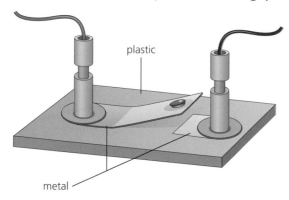

When the switch is closed, the metal parts touch and the electricity can flow through.

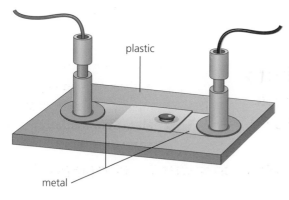

Electrical safety

Electricity from cells is safe to handle but many household devices, such as bulbs, televisions, heaters, fridges and computers, need electricity from a mains supply, which is powerful enough to kill you if not used properly.

In the exam you might be asked about ways to use electricity safely. Here are some simple safety rules:

1 Never use an electrical device that has been damaged.

2 Never use an electrical device near water.

3 Never leave cables and leads from electrical devices trailing where someone might trip on them.

4 Never push anything other than a properly wired plug into an electrical socket.

Keeping us safe

There are various ways in which the design of devices helps us to stay safe. Here are two important ones:

- Plug covers and the coverings on wires and cables are made from an electrical insulator (usually plastic) to prevent electricity from flowing through them.
- Electrical plugs often contain a **fuse**. A fuse has a very thin piece of wire through the centre. Electricity can flow through the wire. If too much electricity flows through, the wire becomes hot and melts. This makes a break in the circuit.

fuse

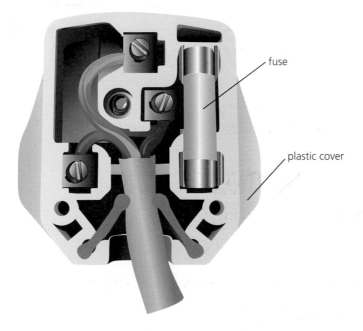

fuse

plastic cover

Try

1 Use words from the box to complete the following sentences.

complete	components	series	terminals

A circuit is a pathway for electricity. The devices in the circuit are known as the ___components___ of the circuit. To make these work they can be connected in ___series___ between the ___terminals___ of the electricity supply so the circuit is ___complete___. (4)

2 Explain how a fuse works.

_____

_____ (2)

Test

Test time: 09:00

3 (a) What is meant by the term 'electrical insulator'?

_____ (1)

(b) Name two materials that are electrical insulators.

_____ (2)

(c) Explain one way in which an electrical insulator can be used to prevent accidents with electricity.

_____

_____ (2)

4 Explain how opening a switch allows you to turn components in a circuit off.

_____

_____ (2)

5 Draw straight lines to join the words in the left-hand column to the correct description on the right.

Words	Definitions
switch	a component that provides electrical energy to a circuit
cell	a component that opens and closes a gap in a circuit
battery	a component that turns electrical energy into movement
buzzer	two or more cells joined together
motor	a component that turns electrical energy into sound

(5)

K: Drawing circuit diagrams

It is important to be able to record electric circuits simply and accurately. To do this we use circuit diagrams. In the exam you may be asked to draw diagrams using the correct symbols for the components. You may also be asked to interpret diagrams and describe how the circuits shown would work.

Drawing circuit diagrams

If you are asked to draw a circuit diagram in the exam it is important to do it really carefully. You may lose marks if the components are not joined properly to make a complete circuit.

You should draw circuit diagrams with a sharp pencil, using a ruler to draw all connections.

We always draw circuits as neat rectangles, even if the circuit is actually a wobbly shape, because this is neater and easier to interpret.

You should draw circuits using the correct symbols for all components. Draw carefully so that there are no gaps in the circuit.

Circuit symbols

These are the symbols that need to be used for 11+ exams.

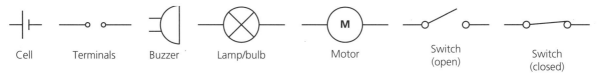

Cell   Terminals   Buzzer   Lamp/bulb   Motor   Switch (open)   Switch (closed)

Drawing series circuits

To draw a series circuit you should draw each component carefully and join them up using neat, ruled lines to make the circuit.

The simplest circuit is one with one cell and one bulb in series.

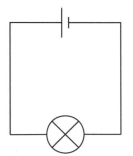

Motors and switches are connected like this:

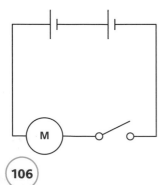

To add another cell, we draw a second cell symbol and join the two cells with a short line. A buzzer symbol is joined into a circuit diagram by the 'legs':

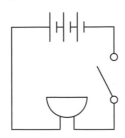

Train

1 Take a sheet of paper and cut it into eight equal pieces. Discard one piece. On each of the others draw one of the circuit symbols. On the back of each one write what the symbol represents. You can use these to test yourself.

Place all the pieces of paper with the diagram upwards. Look at each one and say what it represents. Check by turning the paper over. When you can do this, put them all name side up and use a separate sheet of paper to test whether you can draw each symbol accurately.

Try

2 Draw a straight line to connect each component to its symbol.

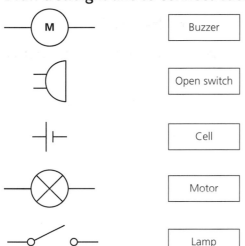

Buzzer

Open switch

Cell

Motor

Lamp

(4)

Test

Test time: 05:00

3 Rebecca has made an entry buzzer for her room. To make it work, she makes the circuit shown here.

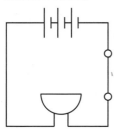

What components are shown in the circuit?

_____ (3)

4 Draw a diagram showing a circuit with two cells, two bulbs and an open switch.

(4)

L: Changing circuits

Changing the types and numbers of components in a circuit changes how they work. For the exam you need to be able to explain how changing the number of cells or bulbs in a circuit will affect the brightness of the bulbs. You also need to know about short circuits and why they are dangerous.

Cells

More or fewer

In a circuit the cells push the electricity around the circuit. If we add more cells, more electricity is being pushed round the circuit and this will make the bulbs in the circuit glow more brightly.

Cell direction

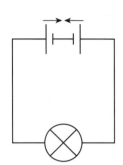

If we have two or more cells, they should all be connected into the circuit the same way round. If one cell is the wrong way round it will try to push the electricity the wrong way.

Turning all the cells round makes no difference to bulbs. They work the same whichever way the electricity is flowing.

Buzzers only work if they are connected the right way round.

Turning the cells round makes a motor turn in the opposite direction.

Bulbs and other components

In a series circuit the energy of the electricity flowing round the circuit is shared between all the components in the circuit.

If we add more bulbs or other components, there are more things to share the energy so each one gets less energy. This will make bulbs dimmer, buzzers quieter and motors slower.

> When working out how changes will affect a circuit in an exam question, it often helps to track the path of the electricity round the circuit diagram with your finger. Start at one end of the cells and move round the circuit, through all the components, until you get back to the other end of the cells.

Short circuits

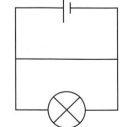

A short circuit is a route that the electricity can take from one terminal of the cells to the other without passing through any other components. This will be an easy route so the electricity can flow round really easily. This has two effects:

- The cells and wires making the circuit can become hot and could cause injury or a fire.
- The cells will run down very fast.

Short circuits are dangerous, so if you connect up a circuit and it doesn't work, your first action should be to check whether you have made a short circuit.

> If you are not sure whether there is a short circuit, do the finger test as described in the previous tip. If you can track all round the circuit from one end of the cells and back to the other without going through anything else, there is a short circuit. Remember that a short circuit will not necessarily be shorter in distance than a safe circuit. Any pathway without a component is a short circuit.

Try •

1 Daniel makes a circuit with one cell and one bulb.

He then makes a second circuit with one cell and two bulbs.

(a) Will the bulbs in the second circuit be brighter, dimmer or the same brightness as the one in the first circuit?

_____ (1)

Next he made a circuit with two cells and three bulbs.

(b) How could the bulbs be made to glow more brightly?

_____ (1)

2 (a) What is a short circuit?

_____

_____ (2)

(b) Why might a short circuit be dangerous?

_____ (1)

Test • • • • • • • • • • • • • • • • • • • Test time: 03:00

3 Look carefully at the following circuits. All the bulbs are off. Explain why the bulb does not light in each case.

(a)

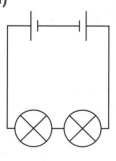

(b)

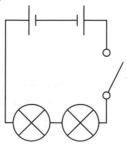

(c)

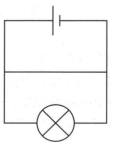

_____

_____

_____

_____ (1)

_____

_____

_____

_____ (1)

_____

_____

_____

_____ (1)

M: The Universe and our solar system

The Universe is a vast place with many billions of objects in it. You need to know the names and relative sizes of some of the objects in the Universe and the units used to measure huge distances. You need to be able to name the planets of our solar system and explain how they remain in orbit around the Sun.

The Universe

The **Universe** is everything there is.

Within the Universe are many **galaxies**. These are huge clusters of **stars**. A star is a massive ball of burning gas.

Many of the stars are **orbited** by rocky or gaseous bodies, called **planets**.

Many planets are orbited by rocky natural **satellites**, called **moons**.

galaxy	satellite
moon	star
orbit	Universe
planet	

> Remember that stars are luminous sources but planets and moons are non-luminous and can only be seen by reflected light.

The distances between objects in the Universe are so huge that even the Sun is over 100 million kilometres from Earth and the next nearest star is trillions of kilometres away.

Our solar system

A **solar system** is a star that is orbited by a group of planets. Our solar system is part of the Milky Way galaxy and our star is the Sun.

asteroid
solar system

The Sun is at the centre of the solar system. The eight planets and many other objects, such as minor planets and **asteroids**, all orbit the Sun. They are kept in their orbital paths by the Sun's gravitational force.

You need to be able to name the planets of our solar system in order. Starting with the nearest to the Sun, they are: Mercury, Venus, Earth, Mars, Jupiter, Saturn, Uranus and Neptune. Mercury, Venus, Earth and Mars are rocky planets. The others are gas planets. Jupiter is the largest. Most of the planets have moons.

How do we know?

Because of the huge distances involved, space objects can only be studied by observation with telescopes. Our understanding is therefore limited by the technology available at any one time.

A number of scientists have contributed to our understanding of how space works. They made lots of detailed observations and recorded them for others to learn from. They thought about their observations and used them to make theories about space. Astronomers (space scientists) do the same today.

You might be asked about how the work of some scientists has helped our understanding. You will be given information about them in the question (see question 3 in the following test for an example) and will not need to remember details of their work. Here are a few of the most important ones.

Ptolemy (Greek, 1st/2nd century). Observed the movements of the stars with the naked eye. He believed that the Earth was at the centre of the Universe. He produced detailed tables of his results that could be used to predict the position of the stars and planets.

Alhazen (Arab, 10th – 11th century). He realised that some of Ptolemy's ideas did not match his observations, but he still believed that the Earth was at the centre.

Copernicus (Polish, 15th century). He proposed a model that had the Sun at the centre of the known Universe.

Galileo (Italian, 16th century). One of the first people to use a telescope. He agreed with Copernicus that the planets orbit the Sun but this view was opposed by church leaders who said that the Bible said that the Earth is the centre of the Universe. He showed that all objects fall at the same rate because of the gravitational pull of the Earth.

Newton (English, 18th century). Best known for working out how gravitational forces keep objects in orbit after he watched apples falling from a tree.

Try

1 (a) Which planet is furthest from the Sun? _____ (1)

(b) The fourth closest planet to the Sun is the one most like Earth. Which planet is this?

_____ (1)

(c) Which galaxy contains our solar system? _____ (1)

2 What is a moon?

_____ (2)

Test

Test time: 04:00

3 Jupiter was known to ancient astronomers but its moons were first seen in 1610 by Galileo. Suggest why no one had spotted these moons before.

_____
_____
_____ (2)

4 All space objects move at great speed through space. Explain why the planets move in a roughly circular orbit round the Sun, rather than in a straight line.

_____ (1)

5 The furthest any human has travelled from Earth is to the Moon. Other places in the solar system are studied by sending space probes or by using telescopes. Suggest why people have never travelled further than the Moon.

_____
_____ (2)

N: Earth, Sun and Moon

Earth is one of the eight planets orbiting the Sun. Earth has one moon orbiting around it. You need to know about the shapes of these three space objects and how they move around each other.

Spheres

The Earth, the Sun and the Moon are all roughly **spherical** (ball-shaped).

> spherical

How do we know that the Earth is a sphere?

Ancient people believed that the Earth was flat like a plate.

Several hundred years ago sailors noticed that, when a ship sailed towards them from a long way away, they could see the masts first, then the sails, then the whole ship, as if the ship was rising up out of the sea.

Scientists realised that this means that the Earth is curved, not flat, and it must be shaped like a ball.

This was proved to be the case when spacecraft took pictures of Earth from space in the 20th century.

How can we tell that the Sun and Moon are spheres?

We see the Sun from every side as we orbit it and the Moon from every side as it orbits Earth. They look circular from every side so they must be spheres.

Movements of Earth, Sun and Moon

The Earth takes $365\frac{1}{4}$ days to orbit the Sun. This is called a **year**.

The Moon takes about 28 days to orbit the Earth.

> axis   day   year

The Earth spins on its **axis** (an imaginary line passing from the north pole to the south pole through the centre of the Earth). The Earth's axis is tilted.

One rotation of the Earth round its axis takes 24 hours. This is called a **day**.

Day and night

The light from the Sun falls on the Earth. Half the Earth is lit and half is in the dark. As the Earth spins on its axis, each part of the Earth moves from light into darkness and back to light.

We can show this on a diagram. You need to be able to draw this diagram.

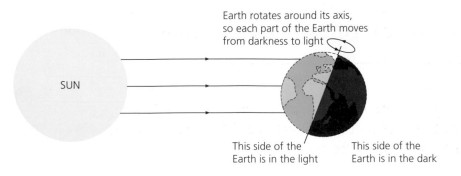

Earth rotates around its axis, so each part of the Earth moves from darkness to light

SUN

This side of the Earth is in the light

This side of the Earth is in the dark

> Notice that the line of the shadow on the Earth runs vertically from top to bottom. It does not follow the line of the Earth's tilted axis.

Changing shadows

As the Earth rotates on its axis, the direction in which we have to look to see the Sun changes. The Sun appears to move across the sky.

The Sun rises in the East in the morning, moves higher into the sky until midday. It then seems to fall lower in the sky until evening, when it sets in the West. As the Sun moves across the sky the length and position of shadows also change.

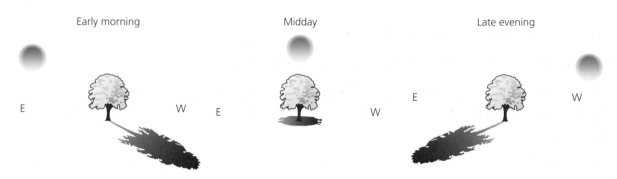

Before clocks were invented, people used these moving shadows to tell the time. A **sundial** is a device that has a part that makes a shadow when the Sun shines on it. The base of the sundial has a scale marked on it. As the shadow moves across the sundial during the day, you can read the time from the scale.

Try

1 (a) How long does it take the Earth to orbit the Sun? _____ (1)

   (b) How long does it take the Moon to orbit the Earth? _____ (1)

2 In the space, draw a labelled diagram to show how day and night are caused.

(5)

Test

Test time: 05:00

3 (a) Using your knowledge of the movement of the Earth, explain how a sundial can tell us the time of day.

   _____

   _____

   _____ (3)

   (b) Suggest one situation when a sundial is no use. Explain your answer.

   _____

   _____ (2)

4 Early people thought that the Earth was flat. Later people believed that it is spherical. These theories were both worked out from people's observations. What happened in the 20th century to prove one of the theories to be correct?

   _____

   _____ (2)

Test 3 Physics

1 Underline the option that best completes the following sentences.

   (a) In circuit diagrams the symbol used to show a buzzer is

   A   B   C   D

   (b) The units used to measure force are

       A   cm   B   F   C   km   D   N

   (c) A material that will be attracted to a magnet is

       A   aluminium   B   copper   C   plastic   D   steel

   (d) A rock casts a shadow because it is

       A   luminous   B   opaque

       C   translucent   D   transparent   **(4)**

2 The diagram shows a spanner being used to turn a nut.

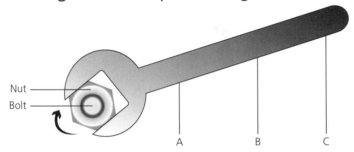

   Nut

   Bolt

       A   B   C

   (a) Which letter on the diagram shows where the effort force should be applied to create the most effect? Explain your answer.

   _____

   _____ **(2)**

   (b) Underline the correct term to describe which type of mechanism a spanner represents.

       • gear   • lever   • pulley   **(1)**

3 Draw straight lines to connect each type of force to the effect that it has on an object.

Type of force		Effect
gravity		attracts a steel paper clip
friction		keeps planets in orbit around the Sun
magnetic		keeps a boat afloat
upthrust		slows a moving car

(3)

4 Lola is watching a trumpeter play in a concert. She hears lots of different sounds.

   (a) Describe how Lola can hear the sounds made by the trumpeter.

   _____

   _____ **(3)**

   (b) The trumpeter plays more softly. How is a quieter sound made on a trumpet?

   _____ **(1)**

(c) The trumpeter plays a higher note. What change has he made in the vibrations to make the note higher-pitched?

_____ (1)

(d) There is a lamp beside the trumpeter. The bulb in the lamp is luminous.

Draw a neat diagram to show how Lola can see the bulb.

(3)

5 Peter has made a model windmill. He makes a circuit with two cells, a motor and an open switch.

(a) In the space, draw a circuit diagram to show Peter's circuit.

(3)

Peter closes the switch. The sails of the windmill turn too fast.

(b) What change can Peter make to his circuit to make the sails turn more slowly?

_____ (1)

6 The diagram shows a system of two pulleys being used to allow a smaller force to be used to lift a heavy load.

Add an arrow on the diagram to show the direction in which the effort force would be applied to lift the load.

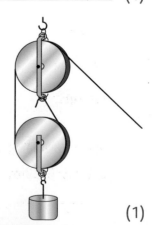

(1)

Record your score and time here and at the start of the book.

Score ☐ / 23   Time ☐ : ☐

Answers

1 Working scientifically

Topic A: Variables and questions (page 11)

<u>Train</u>

1 (a) Yes. This tells us that the surface will be changed and the height of bounce will be measured. (1)
   (b) No. This question does not tell us what variable will be changed or what will be measured. (1)
   (c) Yes. This tells us that the mass on the brick will be changed and the force to make it move will be measured. (1)

2

Question	Independent variable	Dependent variable
How does the temperature of the room affect how quickly seeds germinate?	temperature of the room	time taken for the seeds to germinate
What happens to the distance travelled by a car if the height of the ramp is increased?	height of the ramp	distance travelled by the car
Does the size of a magnet affect how many paper clips it can pick up?	size of the magnet	number of paper clips picked up

(1 mark each)

Topic B: Units, measurement and working safely (page 12)

<u>Train</u>

1 (a) g   (b) cm^3 (c) N   (d) m   (e) mm   (1 mark each)
2 The 0–10 N meter (1) because 9N is closer to the full-scale reading on this than on the 0-100N meter. (1)
3 (a) 4.7 cm (1/2 mark for correct value, 1/2 mark for correct unit). Each small division on the ruler is worth 0.1 cm.
   (b) 52 °C (1/2 mark for correct value, 1/2 mark for correct unit). Each small division on the thermometer scale is worth 2 °C.

Topic C: Testing (page 14)

<u>Train</u>

1 (a) floor surface (1)   (b) distance travelled by the car (1)
   (c) the car used, the height of the ramp, the surface of the ramp, where on the ramp the car is released (any 2 required, 1 mark each)
2 Tamal should use the same mass of sugar (1), the same volume of water (1), the same temperature of water (1) and the same amount of stirring. (1)
3 Select a number of people with different length legs (1). They should all run the same distance on the same surface (2). Compare the times taken to run (1).
4 (a) The distance travelled by a projectile from the catapult/The force taken to pull back the catapult. (1)
   (b) How does the width of the elastic affect the distance travelled by the projectile/the force taken to pull back the catapult? (1)

Topic D: Recording results 1: Tables and bar charts (page 16)

<u>Train</u>

1

Number of marbles	Length of spring, in cm
0	5.0
1	5.4
2	5.8

(1 mark for suitable table neatly drawn, 1 mark each for column headings correctly placed showing variable names and units, 1 mark for data correctly filled in)

2 (a) Axis labels – see bar chart (1 for each label, which should be the same as the column headings)
   (b) Missing bar – see bar chart (1 for bar accurately drawn)

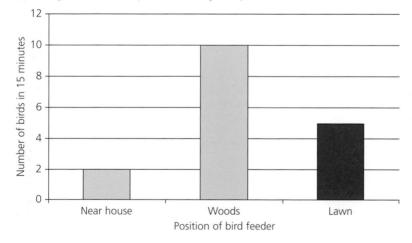

(c) Number of birds seen in 15 minutes at bird feeders in different locations. Allow alternatives that give an indication as to what the bar chart shows. (1 for a title that clearly states what the bar chart shows)

Topic E: Recording results 2: Plotting graphs (page 18)

Train

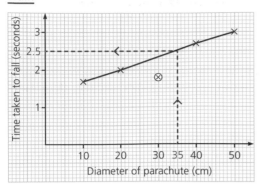

1   Labelled axes – see graph (1 mark each for correctly labelled axes. 1 mark each for suitable scale on each axis).
2   Plotted points – see graph (4 marks, deduct 1 for each incorrectly plotted point).
3   Point for 30 cm parachute correctly circled. (1)
4   Straight line drawn with a ruler through the remaining points. (1)

Topic F: Interpreting graphs (page 20)

Train

1   (a) 2.5 seconds (value correctly read from the graph as drawn). (2)
    (b) Construction lines shown on graph from topic E, 1 for value correctly read
         The larger the diameter of the parachute, the longer it takes to fall.
         (2 marks, allow 1 for the biggest parachute takes the longest or similar)

2   (a) As the time increases, the temperature **increases.** (1)
    (b) As the time increases, the time **decreases.** (1)
    (c) As the time increases, the temperature **decreases** (1) **and then stays the same.** (1)

2   Biology: Living things in their environment

Setting the scene: Life processes (page 23)

1   Answers should make valid comparisons between the two bears. For example:
    ● Both bears have a similar body shape.
    ● Both bears have fur.
    ● The brown bear can move but the teddy bear cannot.
    ● The brown bear can eat but the teddy bear cannot.
2   Answers should focus on how the lack of these life processes would make it impossible for the bear to survive.
    ● **Feed** If bears cannot feed they will not have enough energy for activity. They would not be able to grow or reproduce.
    ● **Move** If bears could not move they would not be able to find food or defend themselves. They would not be able to find a mate and reproduce.
    ● **Grow and reproduce** If bears could not grow, baby bears would never become adults and so they would not reproduce. If they could not reproduce, brown bears would become extinct.

Topic A: Green plants: Structure and growth (page 24)

Train

1   The completed sketch should include the following labelled parts: root (takes in water and mineral salts from the soil and anchors the plant), stem (transports water and nutrients around the plant and supports the leaves and flowers), leaf (makes food for the plant), flower (makes seeds for reproduction).

Try

2   The **stem** is responsible for **transporting water and nutrients.**
    The **leaf** is responsible for **making food.**
    The **root** is responsible for **anchoring the plant in the soil.**
    (3 marks. Deduct one mark for each error.)

3   The conditions needed for plants to grow well are:
    ● enough light to make their food
    ● oxygen and carbon dioxide from the air
    ● water
    ● the right temperature.
    (3 marks, any three conditions required)

Test

4   (a) The flower makes seeds for reproduction. (1)
    (b) The life process taking place in the leaves is nutrition. (1)
    (c) Plants need oxygen as well as carbon dioxide. (1)
5   Answers should be linked to the conditions that plants need to grow well (see Try Q3) and describe an action that would provide a necessary condition. For example:
    ● Water the plants regularly.
    ● Plant them in a sunny position.
    ● Do not plant them outside until there is no risk of frost.
    ● Grow them in a greenhouse to keep them warm.
    ● Ensure a good flow of air to the plants.
      (1 mark each for any two valid answers.)
6   Select two similar plants of the same type. (1)
    Place one in a cold place and one in a warm place. (1)
    Give them both the same amount of water and light. (1)
    Leave them for a week and then compare their growth. (1)

Topic B: Green plants: Nutrition and life cycle (page 26)

Train

1   The four things that plants need to take in from the environment are water (taken from the soil through the roots), sunlight (taken in by the chlorophyll in the leaves and stem), carbon dioxide (taken in by the leaves from the air) and mineral salts (taken in from the soil through the roots).
2   The completed diagram should have the following labelled parts: petal (to attract insects), carpel (contains eggs that become seeds (female part)), stamen (makes pollen (male part)).
3   The four main stages of a plant's life cycle are pollination (transfer of pollen from the stamen of one flower to the carpel of another), seed formation (when the pollen and egg cells join together and become seeds), seed dispersal (spreading seeds away from the parent plant to avoid competition for resources) and germination (when a seed begins to grow into a new plant).

Try

4   Water, light and carbon dioxide are needed for photosynthesis. (1 mark each) (Oxygen, which is made during photosynthesis, is released into the air. Plants need oxygen for respiration.)
5   (a) In the leaves (some photosynthesis also takes place in the stem of many plants but the leaf is the most important site). (1)
    (b) Chlorophyll absorbs sunlight. (1)
6   (a) stamen (1)   (b) light (1)
7   Seeds need to move away from the parent plant to avoid competition (for light and water). (1)

8   (a)   Brightly coloured petals on a flower attract **insects.**
     (b)   In the process called **pollination** grains of pollen from the **stamen** of one flower are transferred to the **carpel** of another by **insects** or the **wind.**
     (c)   New plants can sometimes be made from pieces of root or stem. This is called **asexual** reproduction. (1 mark for each correct answer)
9   (a)   Photosynthesis is the process that provides plants with their food. (1)
     (b)   Animals get their energy from plants because they cannot make their own food. (1)
10   (a)   This seed is wind dispersed. (1)
     (b)   The seed case has wings (1) to catch the wind/hold the seed in the air longer (1).
           (If a different dispersal technique is suggested allow the answer as long as it is supported by a valid reason in part (b).)
11   The quicker germinating seeds may have been planted in a place that had more light/was more sheltered (warmer)/had richer soil with more nutrients. (Allow 1 mark each for any two valid suggestions.)

Topic C: Feeding relationships and adaptation (page 30)

Try

1   Grass → antelope → cheetah. (Allow 2 marks for placing living things in the correct order and 1 for correct use of arrows. Note that food chains should start with a plant and that arrows must be used, pointing from the food item towards the consumer. It may help to read the arrow as 'is eaten by'.)
2   An animal feeding in this way is an omnivore. (1)

Test

3   (a)   For example: seeds → chaffinch → badger and soft fruit → mouse → tawny owl
           (Any two properly constructed food chains using ONLY information shown in the table. For each chain, allow 2 marks for placing living things in the correct order and 1 mark for correct use of arrows.)
     (b)   a predator: tawny owl, badger / fox (1 mark for any one of these)
           an omnivore: badger, fox (1 mark for any one of these)
           a herbivore: chaffinch, mouse (1 mark for any one of these)
4   Sharp beak: allows the eagle to tear meat from its prey (not shown in image)
     Sharp claws: allow the eagle to grasp its prey easily
     Good eyesight: allows the eagle to spot its prey from high in the sky
     (Allow 1 mark for any appropriate adaptation and 1 mark for a valid reason. Two adaptations required.)
5   Plants are the only living things that can produce (make) their own food. (1)

Topic D: Habitats (page 32)

Train

1   The description should be of an animal that would naturally occur in the given habitat and should include appropriate details of size, shape, movement, diet and adaptations to the environment within the habitat.

Try

2   **Migrate** means **travel long distances in search of food or breeding grounds.**
     Hibernate means **sleep through the winter.**
     Nocturnal means **active at night.** (2 marks for all three pairs correctly connected. Deduct 1 for each error.)
3   The tails can be used to grasp the branches/for balance to help them move through the trees. (1 mark for any two valid suggestion.)

Test

4   A habitat is the place where an animal or plant lives. (1)
5   (a)   The woodland must provide food/water/shelter/a safe place to breed. (1 mark each for any three)
     (b)   Dormice might hibernate/eat a lot in the autumn to build up fat reserves/store food. (1 mark each for any two valid suggestions)
6   (a)   Nocturnal (1)   (b)   It is dark at night so they would not be able to see their prey. (1)
     (c)   They would be less likely to be caught by predators/There are lots of moths flying at night/Less competition for food. (1 mark for any valid suggestion)

Topic E: Human impact on the environment (page 34)

Try

1   Pollution means adding materials to the environment that should not be there and might be harmful. (1)

2   Recycling reduces pollution of the environment and reduces use of resources. (1 mark each)

Test

3   (a)   Humans may cut down trees/Replace good tiger habitat with farmland/Reduce prey numbers/Pollute the habitat. (1 mark for any valid suggestion)
     (b)   Endangered species are ones where there are very few individuals left that are in danger of extinction. (1)
     (c)   Humans could protect areas of good tiger habitat/Restore tiger habitat/Breed tigers in captivity. (1 mark for any valid suggestion)
4   (a)   wind/solar/wave/hydroelectricity/biomass (1 mark each for any two)
     (b)   Using renewable energy reduces pollution and slows the use of finite fossil fuel resources. (1)
5   Field margins provide a habitat for animals and plants/provide corridors through which animals can move/Provide food for wildlife/Increase diversity. (1 mark for any one valid suggestion)

Topic F: Animal life cycles (page 36)

Try

1   (a)   Sexual reproduction is a process requiring cells from two parents, one male and one female. (1)
     (b)   Fertilisation is the fusing (joining together) of a sperm and an egg. (1)

2   Gestation (1)
3   There is plenty of food to feed their chicks in summer (1 mark, allow valid alternatives)

Test

4   Similarity: both require two parents cells from two parents. Difference: birds lay eggs and incubate them. Human babies develop inside the mother's body.
     (One similarity and one difference required. 1 mark for each)
5   (a)   Metamorphosis (1)
     (b)   e.g. Frog (no mark is awarded for naming the animal but the changes described must relate to the animal named).
           Tadpoles are shaped like little fish, breathe through gills and live in the water. During metamorphosis they develop legs and lungs and begin to spend more time out of the water. (1 mark each for any three valid changes)

6   (a)   Lots of eggs are eaten so the more there are, the more likely some will survive. (1)
     (b)   There will be competition for food if lots of tadpoles are living close together. (1)

Topic G: Human life cycle (page 38)

Try

1 (a) 9 months (1)   (b) adolescence (1)   2 fetus, baby, child, adolescent, adult (4 marks for all correct, deduct 1 for each error)

Test

3 (a) Girls only: periods (menstruation) begin, breasts develop, hips widen (1 mark, any one required)
   (b) Boys only: voice deepens (breaks), hair grows on face, penis and testes become bigger, shoulders widen (1 mark, any one required)
   (c) Girls and boys: hair grows under arms and around sexual parts, moodiness, spots, growth spurt (1 mark, any one required)
4 (a) 280 days (7 × 40) (1 mark)
   (b) Around 200 – 300 days. Gestation periods are generally longer the bigger the animal. A chimpanzee is roughly the same size as a human. (2)
5 Older people may help with childcare/do voluntary work. (1 mark for any valid suggestion)

Topic H: Evolution and inheritance (page 40)

Try

1 (a) palaeontologist (1)   (b) evolution (1)
2 They can look at which layer of rock the fossil was found in (1). The lower down the layer, the older the rock. (1)

Test

3 Fossils allow scientists to learn about how animals and plants have changed over time/about animals and plants that lived millions of years ago. (1)
4 (a) Offspring all differ slightly from their parents because they inherit a mixture of characteristics from both parents. (1)
   (b) Some changes make the living thing better able to cope in the environment (1) and more likely to mate and pass on the beneficial characteristic. (1)
         Sometimes the changes are so great that a new species is formed. (1)
5 The farmer will select sheep with thick wool and breed them. (1) In the next generation, those offspring with the thickest wool are selected for breeding. (1)
   This continues for many generations until the desired variety is achieved. (1)

Topic I: Classification of plants and animals (page 42)

Try

1 Fungi are not plants because they do not contain chlorophyll and therefore cannot carry out photosynthesis. (1)
2 (a) All vertebrates have a backbone/internal bony skeleton. (1)   (b) Mammals, birds, reptiles, amphibians and fish (5)

Test

3 The mammoth's body is covered in fur. Only mammals have fur. (1)
4 Insects have 3 body parts but spiders have 2. Insects have 3 pairs/6 legs but spiders have 4 pairs/8 legs.
   Most insects have wings but spiders never have wings. (1 mark each for any two differences. Each must mention the features of both groups to make a proper comparison).
5 Reptiles have dry scaly bodies whereas amphibians have smooth, moist skin. Reptiles lay eggs on land but amphibians lay theirs in the water.
   (2 marks for one comparison that uses distinguishing characteristics and mentions both animals)

Topic J: Keys (page 44)

Try

1 B = myriapod   (1)   2 B = mallard   (1)
   C = insect   (1)   C = Canada goose (1)

Test

3 A = fox   B = deer   4 A = ash   B = beech
   C = sheep   D = badger   C = oak   D = sycamore   E = horse chestnut
   (3 marks for all correct, deduct 1 for each error)   (4 marks for all correct, deduct 1 for each error)

Topic K: The human body (page 48)

Try

1 The functions of the skeleton are: 2 (a) Inside the skull (1)
   protection of important organs   (b) Heart and lungs (2)
   supporting the body
   providing a framework for muscles to pull on for movement.
   (2 marks, any two required)

Test

3 A = pelvis   B = backbone   C = shoulder blade   D = collar bone   (1 mark for each correct)
4 Snakes can move more quickly/in a more controlled way than worms because the muscles can pull on the bones of the snake's skeleton but the worm has no skeleton.
   (1 for a difference, 1 for explaining how this occurs)
5 Any two suggestions that show understanding of the three key functions of the skeleton (protection of vital organs, support of the body and framework for muscles to pull on.) (2)

Topic L: Teeth and nutrition (page 50)

Try

1 The four types of teeth are incisors, canines, pre-molars and molars.   2 (a) Vitamin C prevents scurvy. (1)
   (1 mark for each correct)   (b) Carbohydrates provide energy for activity. (1)
                                                                                  (c) Proteins are needed for growth and repair. (1)

Test

3 (a) A balanced diet is one that contains all nutrients in the correct quantities   4 (a) Plaque is a layer of bacteria on the teeth. (1)
        to keep you healthy. (1)   (b) Brush your teeth at least twice a day.
   (b) (i)   Fat stores energy/insulates the body. (1 mark, any one required)   Visit the dentist regularly.
        (ii) Too much fat causes obesity/blocks arteries leading to heart   Use fluoride toothpaste to strengthen the enamel.
              disease. (1 mark, any one required)   Avoid sugary foods and drinks. (2 marks, any two required)

Topic M: The heart and circulation (page 52)

Try

1 (a) Blood vessels carrying blood towards the heart are called **veins**. (1) (b) When you take exercise your pulse rate **increases**. (1)
2 Glucose and oxygen (1 mark each)

Test

3 (a) The function of the heart is to pump blood around the body. (1)
  (b) There are four chambers in the heart. (1)

4

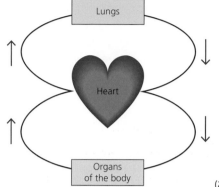

5 Measure your resting pulse rate. (1)
  Take vigorous exercise. (1)
  Take your pulse rate again. (1)
  The pulse rate after exercise will be higher than the resting rate. (1)

(2)

Topic N: The lungs and breathing, smoking and other drugs (page 54)

Try

1 (a) The lungs take in oxygen from the air. (1)
  (b) Oxygen is used in respiration (to release energy). (1)

2 (a) Nicotine is the addictive substance found in tobacco. (1)
  (b) Alcohol interferes with the ability to think clearly/slows reaction time.
      Alcohol may make people become aggressive.
      Alcohol damages the liver.
      (2 marks, any two effects required)

Test

3 The surface of the lungs is greatly folded (1) to increase the surface area
  through which gas exchange can take place. (1)
4 (a) Tar coats the surface of the lungs (1) reducing the area for gas exchange. (1)
  (b) Smoking may cause lung cancer/heart disease. (1 mark, any one required)
5 (a) Addictive substances are ones that it is very hard to stop taking once you start. (1)
  (b) Drugs such as cocaine cause damage to the brain. (1)

Topic O: Micro-organisms (page 56)

Try

1 A micro-organism is an organism (living thing) that is too small to be seen with the naked eye/without a microscope. (1)
2 The three types of micro-organism are bacteria, viruses and fungi. (1 mark for each correct)
3 Bacterial disease: sore throat, food poisoning, whooping cough, typhoid, infection in wound (1 mark, any one required)
  Viral disease: cold, flu, measles, chickenpox, HIV/AIDS (1 mark, any one required)

Test

4 The cowpox material caused antibodies to form in the boy's body (1) and these fought off the smallpox. (1)
5 Antiseptics kill bacteria so cleaning your hands helps to stop the spread of bacteria around the hospital. (1)
6 They could take several identical measuring cylinders (1) and add equal quantities of the bread dough mixture to each (1). They would then place each one in a place
  with a different temperature (1). The one that rises the highest was in the best temperature. (1)

Test 1 Biology (page 58)

1 (a) a herbivore (1) (b) a producer (1)
2 All the food and drink that we take in forms our **diet**. We need to eat a variety of foods to provide all the **nutrients** we need to remain healthy.
  Carbohydrates are a good source of **energy**. There are two types of carbohydrate, starch and **sugars**. We should get most of our energy from **starch**.
  If starch is present this turns from **orange-brown** to **blue-black**. (1 mark each)
3 (a) A is an incisor (1), B is a molar. (1) (b) The skull is more likely to have come from a herbivore (1) because there are no canine teeth visible. (1)
4 (a) Peter's statement is a prediction. (1) (b) The independent variable is the amount of light provided for the plant. (1)
  (c) He should take three (or more) similar plants of the same type. (1)
      He should place one in a dark place, one in a place with little light and one in a place with a lot of light and leave them for a week (or more). (1)
      He should water all the plants equally throughout the experiment. (1)
      He should compare the growth of the plants to see if his prediction is correct. (1)
5 (a) Paul was correct (1). If the tree had no chlorophyll, it would not be able to carry out photosynthesis (1) to make the food it needs to grow. (1)

3 Chemistry: Properties and uses of materials

Setting the scene: Properties of materials (page 61)

1 Response should correctly list any materials used to make the object with appropriate reference to their properties to explain why they were chosen. A 'silly' choice of
  material for the same object should have been chosen with understanding of how the properties of this material make it unsuitable.
2 Diagrams should show how a fair test could be set up, for example with two containers of hot water (same temperature/same volume) wrapped in equal thicknesses
  of the materials and thermometers to measure the temperatures.

Topic A: States of matter (page 62)

Train

1 The diagram should be labelled to show how water **evaporates** from the sea and rises into the air, where it **condenses** to form clouds. Rain then falls and the water
  runs back to the sea in rivers. Over high ground, it might also show the water droplets in the clouds **freezing** to form snow and **melting** at ground level, with the melt
  water running into the rivers.

2   The three states of matter are **solid, liquid** and **gas** (accept vapour). (1 mark for each correct)
3   Accept either difference as below. Both solid and liquid properties should be mentioned to gain 2 marks.
    Solids keep their shape (1) but liquids take the shape of the bottom of the container. (1)
    Solids cannot flow (1) but liquids can flow. (1)

Test

4   Water vapour from the air (1) condenses on the cold window. (1)
5   (a) The freezing point of water is 0 °C. (1)
    (b) Water expands when it freezes (1) so the hose might split. (1)

6   (a) Two places with differing conditions, e.g. one sheltered and one windy, one shady and one sunny, one warm and one cold. (1 for each)
    (b) The water has become water vapour (1) in the air. (1)

Topic B: Solutions (page 64)

Try

1   (a) The solute is the copper sulfate. (1)
    (b) The solvent is the water. (1)

2   Substance A dissolves to form a clear solution so it is **soluble**. Substance B forms a cloudy mixture and does not dissolve so it is **insoluble**. (1 mark for each correct)

Test

3   (a) The dependent variable is the time taken to dissolve. (This is what they measure to get their results.) (1)
    (b) To make a fair test they need to keep the following the same: the temperature of the water, the volume of the water, the mass of sugar crystals used, the amount of stirring. (1 mark each for any three of these.)

4   (a)

Speed of stirring	Time taken for crystals to dissolve, in minutes			
	1st test	2nd test	3rd test	Mean
Slow	6.0	5.4	5.1	5.5
Medium	2.5	3.5	**3.0**	3.0
Fast	1.3	1.7	1.5	**1.5**

(1 mark for each correct)

(b)

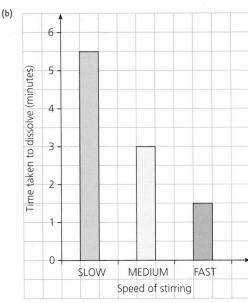

(1 mark each for correctly drawn bar with the appropriate category label added to the horizontal axis. Bars should be neatly and accurately drawn showing the top and sides. Colouring in the bars is not necessary.)

(c) The faster the mixture was stirred, the less time the crystals took to dissolve. (2 marks for a description of the pattern. Allow 1 for answers such as 'The one stirred the fastest dissolved most quickly'.)

Topic C: Separating mixtures (page 66)

Train

1   It is important to be able to draw the diagrams for these two processes quickly but neatly. Diagrams should always be drawn in pencil, using a ruler, and labelled as shown on this topic page.

Try

2   (a) Decanting would be the best method (accept sieving). (1)
    (b) Sieving – the pasta would remain in the sieve and the salt would pass through. (1)
    (c) Use a magnet to remove the iron filings. (1)

3   (a) The material left in the filter paper is the **residue**. (1)
    (b) The liquid that passes through the filter is the **filtrate**. (1)

Test

4   (a) Wear goggles/safety glasses. Do not heat the solution to dryness. (Any 2 required, 1 mark each)
        (The above are the best answers here but accept any other sensible suggestion showing appreciation of the potential hazards in the activity.)
    (b) The salt dissolves/is soluble (1) and so it would pass through the filter paper with the water. (1)
    (c) $100 - 3.5 = 96.5$ g (1 mark for the correct method and 1 for the correct answer. The units (g) should be included, deduct $\frac{1}{2}$ if omitted.)

5   Sieve to remove the wood chips. Add water to dissolve the salt. Filter the mixture to remove the sand. Evaporate the water to obtain dry salt. (1 mark per step. Allow other workable alternatives.)

Topic D: Chemical changes 1: Burning and rusting (page 70)

Try

1 (a) Cooking an egg is **non-reversible**.
   (b) An ice lolly melting is **reversible**.
   (c) A banana ripening is **non-reversible**.
   (d) A pond freezing is **reversible**.
   (e) Toast burning is **non-reversible**. (1 mark each)

2 A fuel is a material that can be burnt to release useful energy. (1)

Test

3 (a) Air (oxygen) and water are both needed for iron to rust. (1 mark each)
   (b) 1. Take two identical pieces of iron (or nails) and clean them. (1)
      2. Place them into containers and add water from the tap. (1)
      3. Add salt to one of the containers. (1)
      4. Leave for a few days and observe to see whether the one with salt rusts more quickly than the one without. (1)
   (c) The paint stops air and water from coming into contact with the metal. (1)

4 (a) A fossil fuel is a fuel that was formed over millions of years/millions of years ago (1) from the remains of dead animals and plants. (1)
   (b) Coal is a solid fossil fuel. (Accept peat) (1)

Topic E: Chemical changes 2: New materials and indicators (page 72)

Try

1 (a) Wood is a naturally-occurring material. (1)
   (b) Concrete is a synthetic material. (Remember that the word 'synthetic' means man-made.) (1)

2 Litmus shows pink in lemon juice (1) because lemon juice is acidic. (1)

Test

3

Material	Natural or man-made	Might be used for
Plastic	**Man-made**	e.g. toys, carrier bags, buckets, gutters (any two required)
Glass	Man-made	Windows, spectacles
Clay	**Natural**	e.g. cups, plates, bricks, roof tiles (any two required)
Wood	**Natural**	e.g. furniture, doors, window frames, toys (any two required)

Allow 1/2 mark for each correct answer.

4 Plant-based materials are sustainable (are easily replaced) whereas oil products will run out/The use of oil products pollutes the environment whereas plant-based materials do not. (1)

5 (a) Chop or crush the berries. (1)   Mix with water. (1)   Boil until the water develops a strong colour. (1)   Filter. (1)
   (b) No, it is not a good indicator. (1) The colours in neutral and alkaline solutions are very similar and could probably only be told apart if placed side by side. (1) (Allow alternative answers if a clear reason is given.)

Topic F: Rocks (page 74)

Try

1 Rocks made up from **crystals** were formed when molten rock from deep inside the Earth cooled.
Rocks made from layers of silt, sand or shells of sea creatures are called **sedimentary** rocks. **Sandstone** is a rock made from layers of sand. **Limestone** is made from the shells of tiny sea creatures.
Fossils are found in **sedimentary** rocks. (5)

2 Rock B is more likely to be made from crystals (because rocks made from crystals are generally harder than those made from grains). (1)

Test

3 Sedimentary rocks are permeable (1) but igneous rocks are impermeable (1). Igneous rocks are hard (1) but sedimentary rocks are softer/more easily scratched. (1)

4 (a) The fossil is unusual because the feathers can be easily seen. (1)
   (b) An Archaeopteryx died and its body fell into a lake/shallow sea (1). Layers of sediment built up over the remains (1). Over millions of years the pressure caused the remains of the animal to become rock. (1)

Topic G: Soils (page 76)

Try

1 (a) Humus is the remains of dead plants and animals (1) that have become mixed into the soil. (1)
   (b) Humus helps to retain water in the soil (1) and contains minerals. (1)

2 Three different soil types are sand, clay contains loam. (1 mark each)

Test

3 (a) Soil A: 15 g + 2 g = 17 g, 25 g − 17 g = **8 g of medium particles**. (1)
   (b) Three bars correctly drawn to show the mass of different size particles as shown in the table (1 mark each). Allow a mark for a bar correctly drawn for the given answer if part (a) is incorrectly answered.
   (c) (i) Soil C is loam (it contains an even spread of particle sizes). (1)   (ii) Soil B is clay (most of the particles are small). (1)
   (d) Soil A would have the quickest drainage rate (1) because it has the largest particles (1) and therefore the biggest spaces for the water to drain through. (1)

4 (a) The soil that allowed the most water to drain through in one minute is the most permeable. (1)
   (b) 1 They should measure the mass/volume of the soil samples accurately to make sure that they use the same quantity for each test. (1)
      2 They should use measuring cylinders rather than beakers so that they can measure the volume of water accurately. (1)
   (c) Impermeable soils may become waterlogged (1) so there is no air in the soil for the earthworms to breathe. (1) (Accept other valid suggestions with a reasoned explanation.)

Test 2: Chemistry (page 80)

1 (a) B An example of a synthetic material is polythene
   (b) C (Different sized particles in a sample of dry soil are best separated by sieving.)
   (c) A (The change of state from a vapour to a liquid is called condensation.)
   (d) D (Feathers are good thermal insulators because they trap air.) (1 mark for each correct)

2 (a) The gate is covered with a layer of zinc (1), which stops air and water getting to the surface of the metal. (1)
   (b) Paint would chip off the chain easily (1) but oil stays on the surface of the metal (1)/oil allows the links of the chain to move freely (1) whereas paint would stick them together. (1) (Allow other valid suggestions comparing the two.)

3 (a) Diagram of filtration apparatus.
    Either of the two shown here.
    Marks: 3 for correct apparatus shown and labelled.
    1 for neat drawing using a sharp pencil and ruler.

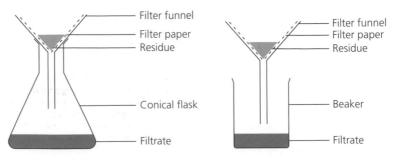

   (b) She should evaporate the water (1). If any material is left behind it shows that there were materials dissolved in the water. (1)
4 (a) The device used to measure temperature is a thermometer. (1)
   (b) The freezing point of a substance is the temperature at which it turns from a liquid to a solid. (1)
   (c) The boiling point of water is 100 °C. (Units must be given as well as the figure.) (1)
5 (a) Burning is a **chemical/non-reversible** change. The wax of the candle is the **fuel**. For burning to take place oxygen from the **air** is also needed. (3)
   (b) The mass of the candle would decrease (1) because the new materials formed/products of the burning reaction are gases (1) and are lost into the air. (1)

6

Liquid	Colour of pink litmus paper	Colour of blue litmus paper	Acidic, alkaline or neutral?
A	pink	pink	**acidic**
B	**blue**	blue	alkaline
C	pink	**blue**	neutral

(4)

7 (a) Granite is hard with large crystals that can be seen without a hand lens. (1)   (b) Sandstone has grains that can be seen but those in shale cannot. (1)
   (c) Slate is made up from thin layers (1), it has no visible crystals (1) and it is very hard. (1) (This can be seen by working back up the key starting from slate.)

4 Physics: Forces, light, sound, electricity and space

Setting the scene: Types of force (page 83)
1 The mnemonic should have nine words beginning in the letters P, P, S, U, M, F, A, G, C in any order. A really good mnemonic will relate in some way to the topic to reinforce the link.
2 Examples include almost all everyday activities. In each case the type of force should be identified and also the effect that the force had on the object.

Topic A: More about forces (page 84)

Try
1 The unit of force is the newton (N). (1)
2 (a) The force pulling everything towards the centre of the Earth is the gravitational force. (1)
   (b) The force stopping you from sinking through the chair is the support force (created by the chair in response to the downward force caused by the gravitational force pulling you towards the centre of the Earth). (1)

Test
3 Four labelled arrows should be drawn (ideally using a ruler) as follows:
   ● Pointing left (forwards) labelled *push from the engine*
   ● Pointing backwards labelled *air resistance*
   (1 mark for each correctly labelled arrow)
   ● Pointing downwards labelled *gravitational force*
   ● Pointing upwards labelled *support force*
4 (a) 7 N   (b) 30 N
   (c) 23 N (1 mark each. Deduct 1/2 for any without the units.)
5 A boat floats because the water creates an upward force (upthrust) (1) that balances/cancels out the downward gravitational force (1).

Topic B: Mechanisms (page 86)

Try
1 (a) The fixed point of a lever is called the fulcrum or pivot. (1 mark, accept either answer).
   (b) Everyday devices that use levers include spanners, scissors, wheelbarrows, see-saws, hole punchers, lever-type door handles, bottle openers; any device that uses a force being applied to a rigid bar or similar turning round a fixed point. (1 mark each for any two suggestions.)
2 A simple **pulley** is a wheel with a rope running over it. To lift a load the effort force is applied in a **downward** direction. Two or more of the wheels linked together allows a **smaller** force to be used to lift the load. (3)

Test
3 The effort arrow should be placed close to the end of the spanner handle, as far away from the fulcrum/pivot as possible and pointing downwards. (2)
4 The back wheel will turn three times for each single turn of the pedal wheel. (2 marks. Allow 1 mark for the statement it will turn more than once.)

Topic C: Friction and air resistance (page 88)

Try
1 (a) Friction is caused when two moving surfaces rub against each other. (1)
   (b) Air resistance is the frictional force caused as moving objects move through the air. (1)
2 The oil enables the two surfaces to move past each other more smoothly (1) thus reducing the friction. (1)

3

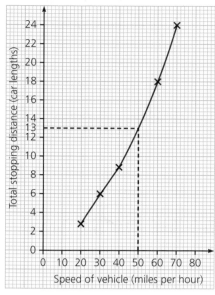

(a) See graph here. Marks awarded as follows
    Axes correctly labelled (1)
    Suitable scale on each axis (2)
    Points correctly plotted (2)
(b) See graph here. 1 mark for a smooth curve linking the points.
(c) See graph here. Stopping distance = 13 car lengths or as shown on the graph.
    1 mark for the correct answer, 1 mark for showing the construction lines on the graph.
(d) The second line should be the same shape as the first (1) but above the original line. (1)
    (Shows understanding that the pattern of stopping distances will be similar but that icy road conditions will make stopping distances longer.)

4   (a) The carpet (1) will allow the shortest travel because its rough surface will create the most friction. (1)
    (b) Air resistance will also act to slow the car down. (1)

Topic D: Magnets (page 90)

Try

1   (a) The force field is strongest at the poles of a magnet. (1)
    (b) (i) Attract (N and S opposite poles attract each other.) (1)
        (ii) Repel (N and N like poles repel each other). (1)

2   A compass needle is a magnet (1) so it will line itself up with the Earth's magnetic field. (1)

Test

3   (a) True (plastic is not a magnetic material). (1)   (b) True (iron filings are tiny pieces of iron; iron is a magnetic material). (1)
    (c) False (copper is not a magnetic material so it is not attracted to a magnet but it will not be repelled because only two magnets can repel each other). (1)
4   The changes will be as follows:
    ● Steel scissors – the reading will increase because the attraction between the magnet and the steel will pull the magnet downwards.
    ● Plastic ruler – the reading will not change because there is no attraction between the magnet and the plastic.
    ● North-seeking pole of a magnet – the reading will decrease because the two north-seeking poles will repel each other and this will push the suspended magnet upwards.
    ● South-seeking pole of a magnet – the reading will increase because the two magnets will be attracted towards each other, pulling the suspended magnet downwards. (1 mark for each correct)

Topic E: Light and how we see (page 92)

Try

1   (a) Light is given out by **luminous** sources. (1)   (b) Light always travels in **straight** lines. (1)
    (c) If light bounces off a **shiny** surface we say that it has been **reflected**. (1)   (d) Eyes can be protected from sunlight by **sunglasses** or **filters**. (1)
2   E.g. Sun, candle flame, light bulb, torch, fire, luminous safety signs. (1 mark each for any two items that emit light)

Test

3   Light from the Sun falls onto the Moon (1) and is reflected from the Moon's surface to Earth. (1)
4   (a) The ray of light should be drawn as a ruled line with an arrow in the centre pointing from the television towards the girl. The line should start on the television and finish on the girl's eye. (2)
    (b) Light from the television enters her eye. (1) The eye sends messages to the brain (1), which interprets the message to form an image of the television screen. (1)

Topic F: Shadows (page 94)

Try

1   **Opaque** means **blocks all light**. **Transparent** means **allows all light to pass through**. **Translucent** means **allows some light to pass through**. (2 marks for all three correct, 1 mark for two correct)
2   A shadow is formed when an opaque object (1) blocks the light. (1)

Test

3   (a) The larger the distance between the object and the wall, the greater the height of the shadow. (2 marks for correct mention of changes in both variables. 1 mark if only one variable is mentioned.)
    (b) As the object moved further from the wall (1) the shadow became less sharp (1) and therefore harder to measure accurately.
    (c) The children could find the average of the three readings (1) and this would make the result more reliable. (1)
    (d) The object was 5 cm high (1). When the object is 0 cm from the wall (i.e. touching the wall) its shadow will be the same size as the object. (2)
4   Similarity: The shadow and the puppet are the same shape. (1)   The puppet has a face (1) but this is not seen on the shadow. (1)
    Difference: The puppet is coloured (1) but the shadow is black/grey. (1)   The shadow is bigger (1) than the puppet. (1)
    (2 marks for any difference mentioning both items)

Topic G: Reflections (page 96)

Try

1 Examples: in the bathroom to assist with make-up/shaving/hair styling; by the roadside to help drivers see round bends; in vehicles to allow drivers to see the road behind them; in shops to help shop keepers watch customers; in cameras to reflect the scene into the viewfinder; by dentists to help them see behind the teeth. (1 mark each for any three valid suggestions.)

2 (a) 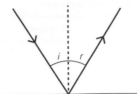 (b)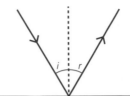

The missing ray should have been accurately measured and drawn so that the angle of incidence and the angle of reflection are equal and marked with an appropriate arrow (1 mark each). In each diagram the correct angles should have been marked with *i* and *r* as shown (1/2 mark for each).

Test

3 (a) You cannot read a book in the dark because it is non-luminous (1) and you cannot see anything unless light from it enters the eye. (1)
   (b) When the light is switched on, rays from the lamp hit the book (1) and some are scattered into the eye (1) so the book can be seen.
4 The diagram should show the two cars with a corner between them. (1) The mirror should be placed so that a light ray from one car is reflected from the mirror and into the eyes of the driver of the other car. (1) The ray should be drawn showing an appreciation that the angle of incidence is equal to the angle of reflection. (1)

Topic H: Sound and hearing (page 98)

Try

1 Sounds are made when objects **vibrate**. Sometimes these movements can be seen but often they are **invisible**. Sounds can travel through **solids**, liquids and **gases** because they are made up from **particles** that can vibrate. (1 mark each)
2 (a) Strings. The harp is a stringed instrument and the strings are plucked to make them vibrate. (1)
   (b) The whole triangle. The triangle is a percussion instrument and when it is struck it vibrates. (1)
   (c) Air inside the flute. The flautist blows across the hole in the mouthpiece of the flute and this makes the air inside the instrument vibrate. (1)

Test

3 The foghorn vibrates to make the sound. (1) The vibrations travel through the air (1) and enter the sailor's ear. (1)
4 When all the air has been sucked out of the jar she will hear nothing (1) because the sound from the bell cannot travel through a vacuum. (1)

Topic I: Changing sounds (page 100)

Try

1 (a) The smaller drum will make a higher-pitched sound than the larger one. (2 marks for making the comparison. Allow 1 mark for the small drum will make a high-pitched sound or similar.)
   (b) Alex should bang his drums more gently to make a quieter sound. (1)
2 B Plucking a string harder will make the sound louder. (1) All the other changes would change the pitch of the sound. (1)

Test

3 (a) The further away she walks (1), the quieter the sound. (1) (Allow 1 for the sound is quieter)
   (b) Robin's statement is a prediction. (1)
   (c) One of them could bang each percussion tube while the other walked away until the sound could no longer be heard (1). They could then measure the distance from the sound source (1). To make a fair test they should bang each one equally hard (1).
4 (a) The thicker elastic band would make the lower-pitched sound. (1)
   (b) The sound could be made higher-pitched by stretching the elastic band more tightly or by pressing down on it to shorten it. (1 mark for either suggestion)

Topic J: Making simple circuits (page 102)

Try

1 A circuit is a pathway for electricity. The devices in the circuit are known as the **components** of the circuit. To make these work they can be connected in **series** between the **terminals** of the electricity supply so the circuit is **complete**. (4)
2 A fuse contains a thin piece of wire that melts if too much current flows through it (1) creating a break in the circuit. (1)

Test

3 (a) An electrical insulator is a material that does not allow electricity to flow through it. (1)
   (b) Plastic, card, wood, fabric. (2 marks for any two non-metallic materials that are insulators)
   (c) Plastic plug covers/plastic insulation on cables and wires (1 for a valid suggestion), stops electricity flowing out of the device into anyone who touches it. (1 for a valid explanation of how the material prevents harm)
4 Opening the switch creates a gap in the circuit (1) so the electricity cannot flow (1) and the components turn off.
5 switch means 'a component that opens and closes a gap in a circuit'.
   cell means 'a component that provides electrical energy to a circuit'.
   battery means 'two or more cells joined together'.
   buzzer means 'a component that turns electrical energy into sound'.
   motor means 'a component that turns electrical energy into movement'.
   (Deduct 1 mark for each incorrectly drawn pair.)

Topic K: Drawing circuit diagrams (page 106)

Train

1 Repeated self-testing should result in the ability to recognise what each symbol represents and how to draw it.

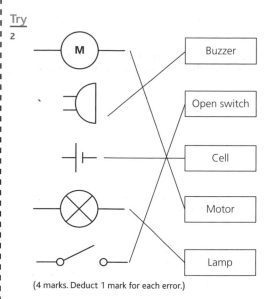

(4 marks. Deduct 1 mark for each error.)

Test

3   The circuit shows three cells (1), a buzzer (1) and a closed switch. (1)
4

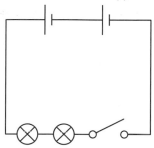

The components can be arranged in any order around the circuit, as long as they are all shown properly connected in series into a single loop.
(1 mark each for the correct symbols and 1 for neat joining up to show a complete circuit.)

Topic L: Changing circuits (page 108)

Try

1   (a) The lamps will be dimmer in the second circuit than in the first (1) (because there are two lamps sharing the same amount of electrical energy).
     (b) The lamps could be made to glow more brightly by adding another cell. (1)
2   (a) A short circuit is one where the electricity can run round between the terminals of the cells (1) without passing through any other components. (1)
     (b) A short circuit is dangerous because it may become very hot. (1)

Test

3   (a) The two cells are facing in opposite directions. (1) (They are pushing the electricity in opposite directions so they cancel each other out.)
     (b) The switch is open. (1) (No electricity can flow through an open switch.)
     (c) There is a short circuit. (1) (The electricity will flow through the easy route and not through the lamp.)

Topic M: The Universe and our solar system (page 110)

Try

1   (a) Neptune is furthest from the Sun. (1)   2   A moon is a natural satellite (1) orbiting a planet. (1)
     (b) Mars is the fourth closest planet to the Sun. (1)
     (c) Our solar system is in the Milky Way galaxy. (1)

Test

3   Jupiter's moons were not spotted earlier because they are not easily seen with the naked eye (1) and telescopes were not available until the 17th century. (1)
4   The Sun's gravitational force pulls the planets inwards. (1)
5   The distance to any other objects in space are so huge (1) that it would take too long to get there. (1)

Topic N: Earth, Sun and Moon (page 112)

Try

1   (a) The Earth takes 365¼ days/one year to orbit the Sun. (1)
     (b) The Moon takes about 28 days to orbit the Earth. (1)
2   The diagram can be checked against the one on this page spread. It should show the Sun and the Earth with the rays of light from the Sun to the Earth drawn with a ruler and marked with arrows. The half of the Earth further from the Sun should be shown to be in darkness, with the line between light and dark running vertically from top to bottom, not along the line of the tilted axis. (1) The dark and light sides of the Earth should be labelled. An arrow should be drawn to show that the Earth is rotating (1) and labelled to show that this brings each part of the Earth from light to dark. (1)

Test

3   (a) As the Earth rotates on its axis (1), the Sun seems to move across the sky. (1) As this happens the position of the shadow cast on the sundial moves across the scale showing the time. (1)
     (b) A sundial is no use at night/on a cloudy day (1) because the Sun cannot cast a shadow (1) to indicate the time.
4   In the 20th century spacecraft were put into orbit around the Earth. (1) These took photographs of the Earth from space, which proved that the Earth is spherical. (1)

Test 3 Physics (page 114)

1 (a) C shows the symbol for a buzzer. (1)
   (b) D: N (newtons) is the unit of force. (1)
   (c) D: Steel is attracted to a magnet because it contains iron. (1)
   (d) B: Opaque objects block the light to form shadows. (1)

3   Links should be made as follows:
   • Gravity: keeps planets in orbit around the Sun
   • Friction: slows a moving car
   • Magnetic: attracts a steel paper clip
   • Upthrust: keeps a boat afloat
   (3 marks. Deduct 1 for each error.)

5 (a)

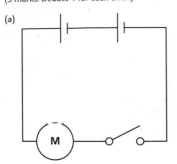

(3 marks: 1/2 each for correct symbols and 1/2 for including two cells, 1 for neatly drawn circuit properly connected up).

   (b) Peter could remove one of the cells to make the sails turn more slowly. (1)

6   The arrow should be shown at the free end of the rope in a downwards direction. (1)

2 (a) Position C would create the most effect (1) because it is furthest from the pivot. (1)
   (b) A spanner is a type of lever. (1)

4 (a) The vibrations from the trumpet (1) travel through the air (1) into Alex's ears. (1)
   (b) A quieter sound is made by blowing more softly/less hard. (1)
   (c) He has made the vibrations quicker. (1)
   (d) The diagram should show Loia and the lamp. (1) A ray of light should be shown by a ruled line from the bulb of the lamp to Lola's eye (1) with an arrow in the middle pointing away from the lamp. (1)

Science Revision Guide published by Galore Park